S0-AXP-992

Mediating Interpersonal and Small Group Conflict

Cheryl A. Picard

The Golden Dog Press
Ottawa – Canada
1998

© 1998 by Cheryl A. Picard

ISBN # 0-919614-81-7

All rights reserved. No part of this publication – other than in brief form for review or scholarly purposes – may be reproduced, stored in a retrieval system, or transmitted, in any form or by any means, electronic, mechanical, photocopying, recording or otherwise, without the prior permission of the copyright holders.

Canadian Cataloguing in Publication Data

Picard, Cheryl A.
   Mediating Interpersonal and Small Group Conflict

ISBN # 0-919614-81-7

1. Conflict management. I. Title.

HM136.P53 1998   303.6'9   C98-900652-2

Printed in Canada.

Layout and Cover Design: The Gordon Creative Group of Ottawa.

Illustrations by Michelle Sutherland.

Distributed by: Prologue Inc.,
                  1650 Lionel-Bertrand Boulevard,
                  Boisbriand, Quebec, Canada   J7H 1N7
                  Tel: (514) 434-0306 / 1-800-363-2864
                  Fax: (514) 434-2627 / 1-800-361-8088

The Golden Dog Press wishes to express its appreciation to the Canada Council and the Ontario Arts Council for current and past support of its publishing programme.

Table of Contents

THE PRACTICE

Chapter Three: Conflict

Chapter Four: Communication

Chapter Five: Mediation

REFERENCES

APPENDIX

This book has been written as introductory text for individuals interested in improving their skills for dealing with interpersonal and small group conflict at home or at work. It is for students learning about conflict resolution and mediation. And, it is a book for "would be" mediators.

Mediating Interpersonal and Small Group Conflict explores the theory and practice of mediation. The book is organized into two distinct sections, one dedicated to the major theoretical tenets of mediation, the other to the practice, skills and strategies used by mediators.

Chapter One discusses the nature of conflict, various conflict styles, the continuum of conflict resolution, as well as the growth and critique of alternative dispute resolution. Chapter Two is an overview of mediation theory. It examines the rise of the mediation movement, various ideologies and approaches to mediation, the process of mediation and role of a mediator, along with some of the issues and trends currently facing the mediation community. Chapters three, four and five highlight the practice elements of mediating interpersonal and small group conflict. Chapter three contains an overview of the key elements of conflict assessment and management. Chapter four describes many of the communication skills used by mediators including reflective listening, effective questioning, reframing, immediacy, bridging and confronting. In chapter five mediation techniques and processes are outlined. Some of these include: conducting an intake, collecting background information, identifying interests, managing the emotional climate, writing agreements, calling a caucus, co-mediation, and hallmarks of an advanced practitioner.

The strategies discussed in this book are based on my learning and personal experience as a mediator over the last twenty years. However, the ideas and skills are not mine alone. The study of conflict and mediation is a burgeoning field and many of the topics and suggested practices found in this book are described in other texts. I have included a list of popular Canadian and American books in the Reference Section under the heading Suggested Readings.

The content of *Mediating Interpersonal and Small Group Conflict* reflects both my mediation model of choice and personal values which I want to make explicit. I believe that mediation has the potential to empower individuals to achieve greater understanding of themselves, each other and the relations that connect them. I also believe mediation has the power to transform oppressive social institutions. And, I believe in most cases mediation is a better dispute resolution process than litigation or other adversarial processes. I identify myself as a relational mediation practitioner which means that I believe individuals are interconnected and possess the capacity for concern of self and others. My style of mediation is facilitative and non-directive.

This book has been a long time in the making. That it is being published now is to the credit of a number of individuals. Firstly, recognition must be given to those who have permitted me to mediate and learn from their efforts to reach understanding and empowerment. Secondly, I am indebted to all those who have been my students. Each of you have helped me to become a better teacher and a more reflective practitioner. Thirdly, I have been stimulated to examine the conceptual issues in the field of mediation by many of my colleagues and by my doctoral work. Finally, and most importantly, I want to acknowledge my family without whose support and encouragement I would not have ventured into this wonderfully rich and diverse profession.

1

The Theory

Chapter 1:

Conflict Theory

The central assumption of conflict theory is that it has personal and social value.

Conflict is an inevitable, pervasive and important aspect of social life. It is generated by differences in ideas, values and beliefs. Although a familiar part of our existence, conflict has contradictory forms, processes, and outcomes. For some, conflict creates enhanced relations, increased productivity and new understandings. For others, it results in dysfunction and disorder. The central assumption of conflict theory is that it has personal and social value – that it serves a function for society. The study of conflict has been undertaken by a range of disciplines; its resolution has become the fascination of a diverse group of psychologists, sociologists, economists and game theorists. The result is a field of study and practice that is both rich and stimulating.

History

Classical thinkers such as Plato and Aristotle viewed conflict as a threat to the success of the state, a view which led to the belief that conflict needed to be kept to a minimum, if not totally eliminated.[1] Seventeenth century philosophers Hobbes and Locke, posited the social contract theory that order was essential for a proper society. In opposition to the belief that conflict was undesirable and harmful, contemporary theorists argue that conflict is as essential to the proper functioning of society as are stability and order. For example, Simmel noted that social phenomena appeared in a new light when seen an angle which included conflict as a positive element; Coser suggested that conflict within a group could help establish or reestablish cohesion; Dahrendorf stated that "not the presence, but the absence of conflict is surprising and abnormal, and we have good reason to be suspicious if we find a society or social organization that displays no evidence of conflict"; and Marx believed conflict was an important aspect of group formation. Coser's book, *The Functions of Social Conflict,* published in 1956, is often cited as the cornerstone of current theories of social conflict. Coser positions conflict as a constructive form of socialization, and posits that a certain degree of conflict is an ally in the formation and satisfactory continuation of group life.

[1] This historical information was found in J. Porter and R. Taplin, *Conflict and Conflict Resolution.* New York: University of America Press, 1987.

Defining Conflict

There is no one definition of conflict. Deutsch defines conflict as "existing whenever incompatible activities occur" (1973:10). Coser gives a fuller explanation; "conflict is a struggle over values or claims to status, power, and scarce resources, in which the aims of the conflicting parties are not only to gain the desired values but also to neutralize, injure or eliminate their rivals" (1968:232). Himes suggests that the way to approach the question of social conflict is to focus on the struggle between the actors. He defines conflict as "the purposeful struggles between collective actors who use social power to defeat or remove opponents and to gain status, power, resources and scarce values" (1980:14). Finally, Hocker and Wilmot define conflict as "an expressed struggle between at least two interdependent parties who perceive incompatible goals, scarce resources, and interference from others in achieving their goals" (1995:21).

Individuals and groups engage in conflict for the purpose of gaining something that is perceived to be in short supply or over needs that appear incompatible. Moore (1986) identifies five causal elements of conflict. These causes include relationship issues, value conflicts, conflicts about interests, discrepancies over factual information, and clashes over structural inequality. Perceived incompatible goals and the perception of scarce resources are central to many conflict struggles. Resources can be physical, economic or social commodities. Tangible resources, such as money, land, jobs, position, are easily identified. It is intangible resources, love, esteem, recognition, respect, that are much harder to identify. Power, status and resources are the leading causes of conflict.

A central element in interpersonal conflict is communication. Communication is the verbal and non-verbal exchange of thoughts and emotions to exchange meaning. How one communicates in a conflict situation has profound implications for the residual impact of the conflict. Communication can exacerbate the situation or lead to productive management. For instance, rigid, insistent communication can defeat the constructive aspects of conflict while open, shared communication can build trust and lead to mutual understanding and productive resolution.

A central element in interpersonal conflict is communication.

The study of conflict is eclectic and multi-disciplinary and gives the appearance of being fragmented. Deutsch (1994), one of the leading psychologists in the study of conflict, suggests that beneath this appearance there are a number of common themes that cut across disciplines and types of conflict. He summarizes these commonalties in a number propositions. First, most conflicts are mixed-motive conflicts in which the parties involved in the conflict have both-cooperative and competitive interests. Second, most conflict can be constructive as well as destructive. Conflict is the root of personal and social change and it is the medium through which problems can be aired and solutions found. The question is not how to eliminate or prevent conflict but rather how to develop the knowledge that will give rise to lively controversy instead of deadly quarrel. Third, within most conflicts the cooperative and competitive interests of the parties give rise to two distinctive processes of conflict resolution – integrative (cooperative) bargaining and distributive (competitive) bargaining. Associated with the different processes are distinctive strategies and tactics for dealing with conflict, differing communication processes, and different attitudes. And fourth, whether the outcome of a conflict will be constructive or destructive depends on the relative strengths of the conflicting parties cooperative and competitive interests.

● ● ● ● ● ● ● ● ● ● ● ●

For conflict to surface, one or more of the parties involved must perceive the status quo as problematic and want to change the situation in which they are interdependently involved.

Conflict occurs within a context of interdependence. For conflict to arise, the actions of one party must affect another; if they do not, differences would exist, but conflict would not (Katz and Lawyer, 1993). Conflict is also a matter of perception. If neither of the parties involved in an interaction perceives the situation to be problematic, then once again there is no conflict. For conflict to surface, one or more of the parties involved must perceive the status quo as problematic and want to change the situation in which they are interdependently involved.

Responding to Conflict

For conflict to be constructive the parties involved must hold a number of essential beliefs. First, they must believe that people can change. In ongoing relationships people usually adjust, accommodate and compromise without loosing their sense of self worth or giving up their needs.

Inflexibility, however, destroys constructive conflict. Second, the parties must believe that allowing a conflict to go unresolved is not acceptable. Third, the parties involved must believe that their view of the conflict may be distorted or incomplete and that understanding the other party's view of the situation is important. In this way, conflict becomes a learning experience that involves asking, sharing, moving, and changing. Fourth, those involved must have the will to find a solution that meets the interests of both parties. This requires focusing on the relational aspects of the conflict rather than on self-interest, and having empathy for the other party. And finally, constructive conflict management is based on the belief that people will try to improve a negative situation if given a fair chance.

Conflict can be influenced by an array of antecedent conditions (Bunker *et al,* 1995). One condition is the physical context which includes such things as location, communication opportunities and time limits. A second condition involves the social context which includes the number of disputants, openness to third-party intervenors or observers, expectations, relationships, and personality considerations. A third condition is the issue context which includes the number of issues in dispute, and the sequencing of the issues.

A number of other factors can influence whether the process of conflict resolution will be constructive or destructive. Some of the factors discussed by Boardman and Horowitz (1994) include the nature of the relationship, the history and power differences between the parties, the perceived significance of consequences, how rigidly the issues are presented, the personal traits and characteristics of the parties, their gender and ethnicity, situational constraints, the inherent conflict management skills of the parties, the various conflict management strategies used, and the extent of diversity in values and attitudes between the parties.

Conflict Styles

Conflict styles are patterned responses that people use in conflict. They are similar to a personality style, although they can be changed. Conflict styles can be viewed as having two dimensions – assertiveness and cooperativeness.

The assertiveness dimension reflects the extent to which we seek to satisfy our own needs while the cooperativeness dimension reflects the degree to which we attempt to satisfy other's needs. Using these two dimensions Thomas and Kilmann (1974) delineated five styles of conflict management, each representing a set of skills which would be useful in certain kinds of situations. Conventional wisdom, for example recognizes that "two heads are better than one" *(collaborate);* it also says, "kill your enemies with kindness" *(accommodate);* "might makes right" *(compete);* "split the difference" *(compromise);* and, "leave well enough alone" *(avoid).*

● ● ● ● ● ● ● ● ● ● ● ●

Individuals who collaborate are both assertive and cooperative, and attempt to work with the other person to find solutions that fully satisfy the concerns of all parties.

According to Thomas and Kilmann, individuals who compete are high on assertive and low on cooperative dimensions. *Competitive* individuals are able to stand up for their rights and defend positions they believe in. They often try to "win". This style is useful when quick and decisive action is vital or when an unpopular course of action needs implementing, for example, in cost cutting or disciplinary situations. *Accommodating* individuals are usually unassertive and cooperative. People who accommodate often neglect their own needs in favour of others' and have a tendency to yield their views. Accommodation is a useful style when a party in a conflict realizes they are wrong, when the issue is unimportant, or when continued competition would damage either the cause or the relationship. *Avoiding* individuals are unassertive and uncooperative, and they typically either side step, postpone, or withdraw from conflict. An avoidance style is useful when the potential damage of continuing outweighs the benefits, when more important issues are pressing, or when it is important to reduce tensions in order to move forward. *Compromising* individuals are intermediate in both assertiveness and cooperativeness. Their objective is to find an expedient solution which often involves splitting the difference. Compromising is a useful style when goals are only moderately important, when the expedition of a resolution is important, or when collaboration fails. Individuals who *collaborate* are both assertive and cooperative, and attempt to work with the other person to find solutions that fully satisfy the concerns of all parties. Collaborating requires exploring the issues to find a creative solution. It is useful when merging insights from different perspectives is important, when concerns must not be compromised, or when commitment must be gained by incorporating other peoples views into a consensual decision. Both conflict management and mediation are collaborative processes.

People's conflict styles often predict their behaviour and communication orientation when in a conflict situation. Individuals are capable of using all five conflict-handling styles. They tend, however, to rely on some modes more heavily than others. Choosing a style for resolving a particular conflict depends on attitudes and philosophy about how conflict should be approached, personal goals and relationships, and the skills available to the people involved (Hocker and Wilmot, 1995:96).

The Conflict Resolution Continuum

People have various means with which to resolve their conflicts. Some approaches include avoidance, informal discussions, mediation, arbitration, judicial or legislative response, along with non-violent and violent action. Each of these options vary with respect to the formality, privacy, authority, people involved and the amount of coercion exercised. Goldberg, Green and Sander (1985) differentiate between primary dispute resolution processes and hybrid processes. Primary processes include adjudication, arbitration and mediation and negotiation, while hybrid processes involve neutral fact-finding, mini-trial, med-arb, ombuds services, and private judging.

Conflict resolution methods can be placed on a continuum with respect to a number of characteristics which distinguish them from adjudicative processes. In the diagram below, those processes on the left give parties the most control, have the most flexibility and privacy, and are the least expensive. As the dispute resolution processes approach the right end of the continuum the relevance of legal norms becomes greater while flexibility, privacy and control becomes less.

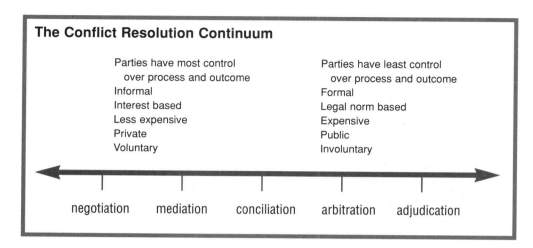

The Conflict Resolution Continuum

Parties have most control
  over process and outcome
Informal
Interest based
Less expensive
Private
Voluntary

Parties have least control
  over process and outcome
Formal
Legal norm based
Expensive
Public
Involuntary

negotiation   mediation   conciliation   arbitration   adjudication

In *negotiation* parties seek to resolve a disagreement or plan a transaction through discussion and reasoned argument. The discussions may be conducted between the parties themselves or through representatives. In *mediation* a neutral third party helps parties to resolve a dispute but does not have the power to impose a solution. *Conciliation* is similar to mediation but the neutral acts as a "go-between" for the parties who never meet. Conciliation can also be defined as the process of bringing parties to a point where they can work out their dispute without the aid of a third party. In *arbitration* the parties agree to submit their dispute to a neutral party who they have selected to make a decision regarding the outcome of the dispute. An arbitrator's decision can be non-binding or binding. Arbitration is used extensively in labour relations because it is less formal, faster and less expensive than the judicial process. *Adjudication* is a formal process conducted by a judge or jury in a court of law. Decisions are reached on points of law, rather than on moral right or wrong.

Alternative Dispute Resolution

Alternative dispute resolution (ADR) represents a move away from adjudicative methods of dispute resolution. Scimecca defines it as "those non-coercive processes which are alternatives to the formal legal or court system" (1993:212). The beginnings of ADR are usually traced back to the 1960's in the United States, and are rooted

Advocates of ADR believed
it would promote compromise
over win-lose outcomes,
replace confrontation with
harmony and consensus,
minimize state control,
and empower communities
to achieve harmonious
resolutions to social
conflicts.

in a desire for harmony, efficiency and access to justice. Advocates of ADR believed it would promote compromise over win-lose outcomes, replace confrontation with harmony and consensus, minimize state control, and empower communities to achieve harmonious resolutions to social conflicts. They sought to minimize the use of professionals in favour of substantive and procedural norms that were common-sensical and non-bureaucratic. In contrast to adjudicative processes, informal processes were to be private, voluntary, consensual and focused on reconciling relationships.

There are two interpretations regarding the growth of ADR in the United States. Some say it stemmed from "grassroots" initiatives led by church, social service and citizen advisory groups motivated to respect the needs of all participants in social conflict. To them, crime was not merely a breaking of laws, it also damaged human relationships. Thus it was felt that attention should be given to repairing social relations, dissolving conflicts and encouraging compliance rather than using coercion. Meaningful change and promotion of new ways to deal with conflict in the community are believed to be some motives of early reformers.

The second interpretation of ADR's development is as a response to an unsatisfactory legal system which had become congested, costly, and serving the interests of the affluent and powerful. Inconsistencies in sentencing, opposition to the conservative view of "just deserts", efforts to minimize stigmatization, alienation of victims from offenders, overuse of the system – all contributed to a "crisis of legality". Deprofessionalization, delegalization and decentralization became the focus of activity of the ADR movement, according to this interpretation of its development.

In Canada, the informal justice movement gained momentum from concerns generating from inconsistencies in sentencing; the alienation of victims from their offenders; and, in the case of young offenders, the influence of labeling theory which sought to minimize stigmatization. The Canadian legal reform agenda of the 1970's resulted in a number of activities being undertaken, the most notable being the repeal of the Juvenile Delinquents Act, and the work of the both the Law Reform and

Sentencing Commissions. In the 1975 Law Reform Commission of Canada report, "Studies on Diversion", the use of ADR was supported based on the conclusion that adjudication was not always appropriate given that the underlying problems of crime were not addressed. The Report went on to say that most of the crimes against persons involved people who knew each other and that the adversarial process contributed to creating a "winner and a loser" which detracted from ongoing relationships. Supporters of informal justice espoused notions of individual and collective empowerment through community mediation and diversion programs. The need for alternative dispute resolution was also supported by criticisms, such as those cited by the Honourable T.G. Zuber in his 1987 Report on the Inquiry into the Ontario Provincial Court System. Justice Zuber found that minor criminal matters were expensive to defend leading some accused to plead guilty, which in turn, led him to suggest that only the very wealthy or the poor on legal aid could afford to go to court. At the time of the Zuber inquiry, delays in criminal courts in some cities were in excess of a year and civil court cases were taking at least that long to reach the pre-trial stage. Courts were seen to be seriously divisive and unable to resolve the underlying causes of crime.

Early ADR initiatives were also an expansion of a philosophical approach to conflict resolution which sought to reduce conflict in the community, maintain better relationships among its members, and bring problem-solving back to the community. Concepts such as alienation and reparation rather than retribution, led reformers to consider ways of bringing victims and offenders together as a means of giving justice back to the community through the restoration of the victims' situation to what it was rather than through punishment of the offender (Wright, 1988). Victim-Offender Reconciliation Programs (VORP) aimed at doing away with court proceedings and eliminating a criminal conviction, while at the same time, making things right between the victim and offender. In 1974, the first VORP in Canada was established in Ontario.

While it is true that some of the ADR movement stemmed from "grassroots" initiatives directed at respecting the needs of participants in social conflict, much of it was characterized by a move away from the adversarial model employed by the legal profession. Legal reformers conveyed their language of dissatisfaction with formal structures and criticized the legal process for being fundamentally alienating. In Canada and the United States, crime was seen not merely as a breaking of laws, but also as damaging human relationships. Alternative dispute resolution programs in both countries had many similar features:

- emphasis on agreed outcomes rather than on strict normative correctness;

- preference for decision through mediation rather than adjudication;

- recognition of the competence of the parties to protect their own interests and to conduct their own defense in a deprofessionalized setting and through a process conducted in ordinary language;

- absence of institutionalized coercion.

Two types of actors supported the development of ADR. On the one hand, community activists espoused the potential for individual and collective empowerment. The Central Mennonite Committee, the Quakers, the Jewish Conciliation Board, and the YMCA each played important roles in the establishment of informal justice programs. On the other hand, legal reformers, faced with problems of legitimization and a dysfunctioning system, saw ADR as an answer to some of their administrative problems. Legal reform also suited the decentralization interests of the government. In the United States the legal sector was very influential in the development of ADR. That influence continues today. For instance, in 1978, the American Bar Association formed the Standing Committee on Dispute Resolution; by 1990 there were at least 157 local or state committees. In 1983, the Harvard Law School established a Program on Negotiation and by 1990, ADR courses were offered in 150 of the 175 accredited American law schools (NIDR, 1992).

ADR was praised for its administrative efficacy. It could offer equal access, act quickly, and allow all citizens to participate in decision making. It was claimed to be faster, less expensive, more accessible and approachable, less coercive and less oppressive, and better suited to tailoring outcomes to the needs of those involved than traditional justice. Informal justice was directed at maintaining relationships, not determining legal right and wrong. It was thought to result in greater satisfaction with resolutions, higher levels of compliance than with adjudicated decisions, and improved capacity for resolving future disputes without external intervention. By using volunteer lay personal and low-paid paraprofessionals, less formal practices were seen as a means of alleviating the fiscal crisis of the state and problems of overcrowding in courts and prisons.

Today, ADR is increasingly being sought as an administrative solution for an overworked court system[2]. This interest is bolstered by the demand for cost reduction by government officials who struggle with declining economies and escalating deficits. In Canada, the Ontario Supreme Court decision in *Askov*[3] put pressure on the province to look for dispute resolution options to reduce court backlogs. In 1994, the Ontario Civil Justice Review was commissioned to develop "an overall strategy for the civil justice system in an effort to provide a more speedier, more streamlined and more efficient structure" (1996:viii). A key component of the 78 recommendations contained in the Commission's *First Report* is that courts would adopt the concept of dispute resolution and integrate alternative dispute resolution techniques. After a successful pilot program in Toronto (Mcfarlane, 1995), it was concluded that referral to ADR was cheaper, faster and more satisfactory; as a result, some jurisdictions in Ontario now mandate all civil cases to mediation[4].

Criticisms of ADR

Critics of ADR suggest that it expands state control (Abel, 1982), that it is a product of the changing nature of state power and form of law (Spitzer, 1982) and, that it re-legitimizes the formal legal system (Harrington and Merry, 1988). ADR is accused of providing "second class justice", a complaint based on the fact that a disproportionate number of clients referred to ADR programs are poor, black and female (Jaffe, 1983; Tomasic and Freely,

....
[2] See, for example, the work of the *Civil Justice Review First Report*. Ontario Court of Justice, 1995 and the *Supplemental and Final Report*, 1996; Hon. T. G. Zuber, *Report of the Ontario Courts Inquiry*. Ministry of the Attorney General, 1987; Report of the Canadian Bar Association Task Force on Alternative Dispute Resolution : A Canadian Perspective, 1989.

[3] See R. V. Askov [1990] 2 S.C.R. 1199.

[4] In June of 1997, the Ontario Ministry of the Attorney General proposed a new rule (Rule 78) to provide for the mandatory mediation of most civil actions and applications.

1982). ADR is also criticized for creating more institutions of political control than empowering alternatives (Hofrichter, 1987). In addition, there are complaints of legal rights violations, exploitation, coercion, and expansion of state control into private lives (Kressel, *et al,* 1989). Thus, it is said, only formal procedures, based on rules of evidence, can require compliance with decisions, and only legalism can protect the less powerful (Roel and Cook, 1989). Further, informal practices were faulted for not living up to their claims of reducing the burden and size of the legal apparatus, and were accused of widening the net of social control. Harrington's (1985) work, which pointed out that few of those referred to mediation would ever have had a court hearing, supported this conclusion. Although it was agreed that ADR was more humane, responsive, and participatory, opponents argued that it marginalized certain crimes and did not have any long-range impact on the distribution of power or on the high cost of the legal system. Other lines of attack saw informalism as augmenting oppression by reinforcing patriarchal and middle-class values and by increasing state power (Abel, 1982). Informal dispute resolution processes were believed to suppress social conflict through the rhetoric of harmony ideology (Nader, 1991). ADR was accused of being susceptible to domination by stronger parties, and programs were criti- cized for diverting resources and attention from needed court reforms. ADR was deemed inadequate, and despite its flaws, the courts were said to remain the best providers of justice.

While the ideals of ADR may not have been fully borne out, it is fair to say that in a relatively short period of time alternatives to the traditional trial have become a significant factor in modern day dispute resolution. As ADR continues to grows in popularity, advocates will no doubt continue to seek to improve its procedures and techniques.

Of all of the ADR processes, mediation has received the most attention and is said to have emerged as the single most powerful tool in the alternative dispute resolution movement (Bush and Folger, 1994). Before moving to a discussion of mediation as a key dispute resolution process, it is prudent to say a few words about conflict and culture.

Conflict and Culture[5]

Recent research in the field of conflict studies has focused on the links between conflict and culture. Culture, in this instance, refers to race and ethnicity; although when broadly defined, it can include gender, age, socioeconomic status, sexual orientation, educational levels and physical ability. Culture helps to create a system of meaning that must be understood in order to contextualize conflict, identify the parties involved in a conflict, determine how to approach and enter a conflict, and recognize how the conflict is best resolved. While culture alone does not determine individual behaviour in conflict, it does shape the ways in which conflict is viewed, discussed and resolved (Avruch & Black 1993).

Culture provides a "lens" through which conflicts are perceived and interventions or reactions are developed. Some of the issues that arise when cultural analyses are applied to conflict include the following. What constitutes a conflict is the starting point for a cultural understanding of conflict. While denial or avoidance of conflict seems to be common across all cultures, it is extreme in those cultures that privilege harmonious over conflictual conceptions of the world. Parties to a conflict can include those directly affected by events, as well as those indirectly affected. Cultures where individuals see themselves as members of groups, such as families, clans or communities, tend to consider all members of their group when they assess the impact of conflict and its favoured outcome. Approaches to conflict and preferred intervention styles also vary depending upon the culture. Some cultures prefer direct and open confrontation, while others rely on third parties to delicately broach the subject of contention, without joint sessions, in order that both parties can save face. If intervention is preferred, who intervenes becomes a question. Should the intervenor be someone close to and knowledgeable about both parties, or a "neutral and impartial" stranger? In some cases, intervention may not be perceived as the best strategy, since the conflict may improve over time without any attention. Finally, culture will influence how a resolution is understood as fair and equitable. In addition, the formality of resolution will be shaped by its cultural context.

G. Hofstede (1980) has developed a spectrum of cultural differences for understanding workplace patterns of behaviour. This spectrum, modified here, is based on dimensions of

....
[5] With permission from R. Ramkay.

differences that are specific to cultures, such as whether individualist-collectivist identities are evident; high-low tolerance for ambiguity, whether change is tolerated; high-low power distance, where hierarchies and traditions are either rigid or flexible; and masculine-feminine values, whether nurturing or assertive behaviours are common. These constructs are reflective of patterns for processing information and evaluating events within a cultural context.

When working in intercultural conflict resolution, several challenges face the intervenor. The first is establishing connections with the parties in dispute in order to enter the conflict. An intervenor must establish the trust and confidence of the parties. This can result in lengthy meetings to talk about the situation, where the conflict itself does not come up for discussion until many hours have passed and the party or parties have developed confidence in the intervenor. In the second instance, once trust is established, the intervenor needs to show some authority in her or his intervention. The parties in conflict need to believe that the intervenor can help influence the other party and assist in settlement. Thirdly, the intervenor must recognize the possible involvement of others not directly involved in the dispute and invite or encourage them to participate in its resolution. The fourth consideration for the intervenor might be the parties' disinterest in face to face confrontation. The intervenor may be required to assist through a conciliation model, as opposed to a joint session of mediation. John Paul Lederach (1982) proposes that a more elicitive model of conflict intervention be developed in conjunction with the disputing parties. Instead of prescribing a particular model of conflict resolution for the parties, the intervenor might need to construct a new model, with the parties' input, in order to assist in resolution. Finally, the intervenor should expect flexibility with respect to the formality of the agreement. Under no circumstances, should a conflict intervenor expect a formal, written agreement. This may not be desired by the parties.

While intervening in conflict where cultural differences are evident, an interactive analysis of the conflict and an exploration of resolution methods must be undertaken with the parties to the conflict. Intervenors should expect differences and adopt flexible procedures.

Mediation is an alternative dispute resolution process in which a third party helps the parties in dispute resolve the situation by coming to their own solutions. Mediation is not a new concept. However, a new surge of interest in its use has brought mediation to the fore of modern dispute resolution practice. Increasingly mediation is being used in an array of social and legal venues. There are those who believe mediation presents a powerful opportunity to express and achieve a higher vision of human life. The more dominant approach, however, emphasizes mediation's capacity for finding solutions that are expedient, less costly and more satisfying than formal adjudicative processes. Whichever perspective is taken, it is agreed that mediation is both diverse and pluralistic and that no one approach or ideology represents the "full story" of mediation.

• • • • • • • • • • • •

Mediation is one of the oldest and most common forms of conflict resolution.

History

The history of mediation is entwined with the core values of Canadian society, most notably justice, self-determination, and the acceptance of humans as rational, problem-solving beings. Rooted in social activistism, early proponents of mediation sought to assist individuals and groups to use non-violent and more effective problem-solving strategies, the hope being that informalism would return justice to the community. While mediation in labour disputes has been long used[6], it was not until the 1960's that mediation realized wider acclaim in the realms of community, family, and public policy, and legal contexts. Increasingly, mediators are being called upon to resolve disputes about child custody, contracts, environmental concerns, neighborhood problems, and playground bullying.

Mediation is one of the oldest and most common forms of conflict resolution. Its current practice has evolved from that which existed in other countries and other times. For example, the Bible refers to Jesus as a mediator between God and man. Jewish rabbinical courts and rabbis in Europe were vital in mediating disputes (Moore, 1986). In ancient China, mediation was the principle means of resolving

• • • • • • • • •
6   Since the early 1900's, both labour and management have routinely appealed to neutral third parties as a method by which grievances can be reasonably settled.

disputes. It has a rich history in Japanese law and customs. In parts of Africa the *moot,* or neighborhood meeting, has long provided an informal mechanism for resolving interpersonal disputes (Folberg and Taylor, 1984). Early Native American tribal cultures, including Navahos and Lakotas, used mediation to resolve disputes (Garrett, 1994). Legal anthropologists, convinced of the advantages of informalism based on the experience of comrades courts in Russia, people's courts in China and community courts in South America, argued that they demonstrated both the "naturalness" and the "universality" of informal dispute processing (Auerbach, 1983). Extended families, elders, clan members, and religious leaders have all offered wisdom, precedent, and models to assist in the resolution social conflict. With the rise of nation-states, mediators have taken on new roles as secular diplomatic intermediaries.

Much of what is known about the historical roots of mediation tells us that it has grown out of strong moral and social concerns. Early practitioners of the modern Western era were attracted to mediation for the betterment of society, albeit with differing motives. Social activists were interested in community empowerment. Legal reformers sought legal equality and access to justice. Church groups (especially the Mennonites and Quakers) were interested in reconciliation and restoration of harmony. Peace activists were drawn to collaborative problem-solving by their concern about nuclear war and global destruction.

Early mediation programs in Canada evolved from court-based programs that were ideologically linked to restorative justice. The first Victim Offender Reconciliation Program (VORP) was started in 1974 in Kitchener, Ontario, and by the late seventies, court-based mediation programs existed in Halifax, Quebec City, Montreal, Winnipeg and Regina (Lajeunesse and Woods, 1987). One of the first community-based mediation programs, now called Community Justice Initiatives, was established in 1978 by the Central Mennonite Committee in Ontario. Community mediation was dominated by a therapeutic model which emphasized consensus rather than coercion, integration rather than exclusion, and mutually satisfying outcomes rather than strict observation of legal rules. Harrington and

Merry (1988) identified three analytically distinguishable streams within the community mediation movement; the delivery of dispute resolution services, personal growth and development, and social transformation. The *delivery of service* stream saw the courts as inefficient, inaccessible and inappropriate for many kinds of disputes, and had as a primary interest the rationalizing, streamlining and fine-tuning of the judicial system. The *personal growth* stream envisioned consensual dispute settlement empowering individuals to take greater control over their lives by enhancing their personal skills for dealing with conflict. The *social transformation* stream centered on community empowerment through decentralized decision-making, deprofessionalized dispute resolvers and local rather than state control systems. Each stream held different political interests, developed different organizational models, and was active in different spheres. In the end, Harrington and Merry believe the service delivery stream won out over the other two.

> **The use of mediation has come to be regarded as a legitimate means to deal with many social and legal conflicts In Western society.**

In a relatively short period of time, the use of mediation has come to be regarded as a legitimate means to deal with many social and legal conflicts in Western society. Mediation now commands the attention of scholars, researchers and legislators. New journals and books appear on the bookstands on a regular basis. Professional associations boast large memberships. Universities offer graduate and undergraduate degree programs in conflict resolution and mediation and professional conferences abound. Corporations and individuals from a variety of occupations have responded to the growing demand for non-adversarial dispute resolution. In 1995 more than five thousand dispute resolution professionals were known to exist in Canada (Department of Justice, 1995).

Four "stories" characterize the mediation movement – the Satisfaction Story, the Social Justice Story, the Oppression Story, and the Transformation Story (Bush and Folger, 1994). According to the *Satisfaction story,* mediation facilitates collaborative problem-solving rather than adversarial distributive bargaining. It is seen as a powerful tool for satisfying human needs, and has led to more efficient use of private and public dispute resolution resources. The *Social justice story* tells of mediation helping to form effective grassroots community structures by reducing dependency on professionals and empowering individuals to participate in civic life. According to the *Transformation story,* participation in mediation helps individuals gain a greater sense of self-respect, self-reliance, and self-confidence. It strengthens their inherent capacity to acknowledge their concern for each other as human beings and promotes individual moral development. Finally, the *Oppression story* tells the tale of mediation that produces outcomes which favour the stronger parties by ignoring or undermining the efforts of weaker parties. This version of mediation sees it as neutralizing social justice gains by helping to reestablish the privilege of the stronger class and perpetuating the oppression of the already disadvantaged.

Defining Mediation

The word mediation is derived from the Latin words *medi* or *medio* which means middle. In its simplest form, mediation can be defined as a process of assisted or facilitated negotiation where the mediator controls the process and the parties determine the outcome. It provides third-party assistance to individuals trying to reach agreement in a controversy. Mediation involves the intervention of a "non-partisan third party, whose authority rests on the consent of the parties to facilitate their negotiations; a mediator has no independent decision-making power beyond what the parties afford" (Mcfarlane, 1997:2). The central quality of mediation is said to be:

> it's capacity to reorient the parties towards each other, not by imposing rules on them, but by helping them to achieve a new and shared perception of their relationship, a perception that will redirect their attitudes and disposition toward one another (Fuller, 1971:325).

• • • • • • • • • • • •

Mediation can be defined as a process of assisted or facilitated negotiation where the mediator controls the process and the parties determine the outcome.

Edward Kruk, sets out a number of key principles in his definition of mediation:

> [Mediation is] a collaborative conflict resolution process in which two or more parties in dispute are assisted in their negotiation by a neutral and impartial third party and empowered to voluntarily reach their own mutually acceptable settlement of the issues in dispute. The mediators structure and facilitate the process by which the parties make their own decisions and determine the outcome, in a way that satisfies the interests of all parties in the dispute (1997:4).

Following from Kruk's definition, the core components of mediation are that:

- it is a *process* with defined stages;
- it is used in situations where there is a *disagreement* between two or more parties;
- through *collaboration,* solutions reached in mediation benefit everyone;
- the mediator remains *neutral and impartial* and has no vested interest in outcomes;
- parties are *empowered* to make their own decisions;
- parties enter into mediation *voluntarily,* without coercion or control.

Mediation is eclectic and multi-disciplinary. Its development, and now its study, have been undertaken in the fields of anthropology, communications, economics, political science, psychology, law, management, and industrial and international relations. Mediation is used in a variety of forums including the courts, business, schools and institutions of higher education, neigbourhoods, families, and organizations. Mediation is used to resolve public policy and environmental issues, landlord-tenant and congregational conflicts, farmer-lender negotiations, international and cross-cultural conflicts, and medical malpractice suits. Although it could be even more widely used, mediation is not a panacea. It should not be used when one party appears to be more interested in winning than collaborating, when the interests of one party cannot be fully represented, or, when one party would be placed in danger through his or her participation. Mediation should also not be used as a substitute for therapy or counseling, as a coercive means to an end, as a substitute for the proper exercise of authority, when competent mediators are unavailable, when power should not, or cannot, be balanced, or, when the goal is repressive. A useful caveat to remember is that *"parties who participate in mediation should never leave worse off than when they came"*. Knowing when to use mediation and for what purpose is critical to the successful resolution of disputes.

The Process of Mediation

Mediation processes differ widely. Common to most is that outcomes are consensual, rather than imposed, and that solutions are fashioned by the parties themselves through a process of direct negotiation. It is important that mediation be flexible and able to meet the needs of particular individuals and situations. This means that the more commonly used Western model of mediation described in this book may not always be appropriate, especially in cases involving cross-cultural and intercultural disputes. This has become evident in recent research which shows that people of colour fare poorly in comparison to their white counterparts in mediation, except in cases where the mediators are of the same ethnic group (LeBaron, 1997). Mediators must be both flexible and skilled enough to recognize when the mediation process requires adaptation.

Mediation has three distinct phases – a beginning, where the issues and key parties to the dispute are identified; a middle, where the interests underlying the positions are articulated; and an end, where options are generated, evaluated, and agreed upon. In this text the process of mediation is organized into five distinct stages. In stage one, *introduction of the process,* the mediator describes the process and the mediator's role, sets a collaborative tone, outlines a protocol for communication, discusses the parties authority to settle and explains the limits of confidentiality. Stage two, *identification of the issues,* provides an opportunity for parties to begin to tell their story, why they came to mediation, and what issues they are hoping to discuss. Stage three, *exploration of the interests,* is the heart of the mediation process. This is when interests are uncovered, when issues are broadened to reveal emotions, and when parties begin to understand what is motivating them as well as what is important for the other party. Stage four, *generating solutions,* has the parties brainstorm multiple options. And stage five, *reaching an agreement,* is when the parties select from the options those which meet their mutual interests and are realistic. At the conclusion of the mediation an agreement may be written and signed by the parties, or, with their consent the mediator may draft an agreement outside of the mediation to be viewed by the parties and their lawyers, then signed at a later date.

• • • • • • • • • • •

Uncovering interests is the heart of mediation; it is where the "magic of mediation" occurs.

Fisher and Ury's (1981) classic text, *Getting to Yes,* sets out one of the fundamental principles of negotiation, that of shifting people from their *positions* (their wants), to their *interests* (their needs). Fisher and Ury define this activity as one of principled-based bargaining, in contrast to positional-based bargaining. Principled bargaining is a method of negotiation designed to produce wise outcomes efficiently and amicably. It is comprised of four key elements; separating the people from the problem, focusing on interests, rather than positions, inventing options for mutual gain, and insisting on objective criteria.

As noted, uncovering interests is the heart of mediation; it is where the "magic of mediation" occurs. Interests are the underlying needs that cause a person to take a particular position and make demands in a negotiation. Interests are of three broad types; substantive, procedural and psychological. *Substantive interests* refer to tangibles such as money and time; procedural interests are preferences for the manner in which decisions are to be made, and psychological interests refer to the emotional and relationship needs of each party. For example, a positional statement might sound like, *"promote me or I will start looking for a new job,"*; an underlying interest for this demand may be the need for more recognition or higher pay to finance the purchase of a larger home. Inherent in interest-based negotiation is the belief that in many conflicts, an exami-

A successful mediator is
one who is able to uncover
the factual as well as
emotional elements
contributing to a dispute.

nation of the underlying interests reveal the existence of more concerns that are shared and compatible than opposed. Shared needs in the above scenario might include the employee wanting to continue working for the company, and the company not wanting to loose a good employee – both parties therefore have a shared interest in finding a satisfactory solution to the stated problem of wanting a promotion. Disputants often have not previously talked about their interests with one another, and may not have consciously articulated their needs to themselves. A successful mediator is one who is able to uncover the factual as well as emotional elements contributing to a dispute, who is able to reframe these as needs and interests, some of which are likely to be in-common and shared by the parties, and who is then able to help the parties seek integrative and mutually agreeable solutions that meet individual interests. While uncovering interests is not the only work of a mediator, it is often the hardest because of the elusive nature of interests. One way of probing for interests that has proved helpful is to think of interests as CHEAP BFV's. That is, interests are the concerns, hopes, expectations, assumptions, priorities, beliefs, fears and values of each party. Asking CHEAP BFV questions can help to uncover the interests giving rise to a conflict.

Another cornerstone of effective mediation is that of good communication. Good communication involves a mediator putting aside their own views and feelings in order to help the parties listen to and understand each other. Listening is an important learned skill; it accounts for the majority of work done by a mediator in a mediation. The strategic use of communication "tools" such as reflective listening, reframing, questioning and confronting, are essential to successful mediation.

For the most part, mediators make use of joint, face-to-face sessions, however, in some circumstances private meetings, or caucuses, are used to help uncover resistance to communication between the parties and promote movement toward an agreement. Caucuses allow strong feelings to be expressed in private, help the mediator determine if there are mediator-party issues which should be addressed, allow a breather or cooling off period, and allow parties to discuss options while not under the scrutiny of the other party. Caucuses are also important in that they allow for the exploration of fears and possible threats that could not be discussed in face-to-face meetings.

The Role of a Mediator

There is no clear consensus on the role of a mediator. Differences in background, training and professional discipline, as well as area of practice are reflected in competing views of what it is that mediators do. One view is that a mediator is an active but neutral facilitator. Some of the tasks performed by a mediator involve structuring the process, managing emotions, organizing information, facilitating communication, helping parties to develop and evaluate solutions, and producing a written agreement. Mediators play a number of roles including that of catalyst, communicator, educator, translator, expander of resources, bearer of bad news, agent of reality, protector of the process, and in some cases, scapegoat. To serve these functions, a mediator should be capable of appreciating the dynamics of the environment in which the dispute is occurring; be an intelligent and effective listener; be articulate, patient, non-judgmental, flexible, forceful and persuasive, be imaginative and resourceful; be a person of professional standing or reputation; be reliable and capable of gaining access to necessary resources; be non-defensive and a person of integrity, as well as be humble, objective and neutral with regard to the outcome of a dispute (Stulberg, 1987).

• • • • • • • • • • •

Until quite recently, mediation has been considered more an art than a science.

Approaches to Mediation

Up until quite recently, mediation has been considered more an art than a science. Early mediation approaches were described as being either *content interventions* (which focus on substantive issues), or, *process interventions* (which focus on communication and relationship issues). The common practice when classifying approaches to mediation has been to situate them as polar opposites. For example, Schwerin (1995) classified interventions as contrasting schools of thought about a mediators' role — one as facilitator, the other as activist. Riskin (1996) described mediators as being either facilitative or evaluative. Bush and Folger (1994) contrasted transformative and problem-solving styles, and Kolb (1983) labeled the different functions of a mediator as dealmaker or orchestrator. Others authors use binary classification schemes including broad versus narrow, principled versus interest-based, settlement versus recognition, problem solving versus adversarial, and facilitative versus evaluative.

One of the early studies on what it is that mediators do was carried out by Silbey and Merry (1986) who constructed a typology consisting of two ideal-type descriptions of mediator approaches – the bargaining style and the therapeutic style. They differentiated the two styles on the basis of how mediators present themselves and the mediation process, how they control the process, and the control they have over the substantive issues to be mediated. In their view the bargaining style reflects a greater measure of control of the process and focuses on settling the dispute based on what parties "want", while the therapeutic model focuses less on settlement and more on communication and relationships.

A more recent, and controversial, account of mediation approaches has been put forward by Bush and Folger (1994) in their book, *The Promise of Mediation.* Similar to Silbey and Merry, Bush and Folger describe mediation as having moved toward a form that encompasses a directive and problem-solving approach where reaching agreement is paramount. They contrast the directive approach with a transformative model of mediation that gives individuals a greater sense of their own efficacy and a greater openness to others. Bush and Folger suggest that as mediation has developed, the problem-solving potential of mediation has been emphasized to such an extent that a directive, settlement driven model of mediation has become the more dominant form of practice.

Other authors have posited mediation approaches as dichotomous. For example, Kolb et al (1994) used the metaphor of "framing" to characterize the interpretive schemes that mediators used to make sense of and organize their activities. They based their study on twelve influential mediators from different sectors which included family, divorce and child custody, special education, environmental, labor, community, international, business, public policy and public housing. What they found was that two primary frames, settlement and communication, reflected the tendency of mediators to define their roles and structure their activities. Those mediators whose role was framed as settlement tended to work toward uncovering the elements of a possible deal and to convincing the parties to accept the deal. Mediators whose frame was characterized as enhancing communication worked to keep the parties talking so that they could better understand their conflict. Reaching a settlement was considered secondary to attaining mutual understanding. Settlement mediators were directive and took an activist view of the role of a mediator. Communicative mediators were less directive, seeing their role as the "orchestra leader" who influenced the ways parties talked, how issues were framed, the way problem was understood, and the flow of information. Although frames translated into specific actions, Kolb suggests that they do not appear to be preset and often reflect on the spot decision making. Her conclusion is consistent with Carnevale et al's (1989) work which confirmed that mediation strategies are contingent upon how mediators perceive their role.

A number of the categorizations used to distinguish a mediator's approach make reference to social norms. This observation led Waldman (1996) to devise a typology which focused explicitly on the role of social norms in mediation. Her typology includes three mediation models: norm-generating, norm-educating, and norm-advocating. While each of the models share common assumptions, procedural routes, and mediative techniques, they have distinguishing features. The norm-generating model is inattentive to social norms and seeks above all else to give maximum autonomy to the disputants. The norm-educating model is premised on the belief that knowledge of social norms is a precondition to autonomous decision making. In the norm-advocating model the mediator not only helps parties reach an agreement that satisfies their individual needs, he or she also assumes responsibility for ensuring societal principles are included in the agreement.

The approach used by a mediator is influenced by his or her past experience, training and ideology as well as the context in which mediation takes place.

Different visions of what mediation is, and what it should do, make it difficult for people to select between mediation and other dispute resolution processes, as well as to determine who is best able to mediate their disputes. Riskin (1996) responded to this problem by proposing a system for classifying mediator orientations. His grid for evaluating the character of mediation styles emphasizes two features: how mediators view the role of the mediator (evaluative or facilitative); and, how mediators define the conflict to be resolved (narrow or broad). An evaluative-narrow approach to mediation practice would involve a mediator assessing the strengths and weaknesses of parties' claims, predicting court outcomes, developing and proposing a settlement and pushing parties to settle based upon his or her assessment. An evaluative-broad perspective also seeks settlement but uses a process which emphasizes interests over positions, with the mediator's proposed solutions attempting to accommodate these interests. A facilitative-broad approach helps the parties understand and define the problems they wish to address and facilitates a discussion of underlying interests rather than positions. It helps them generate and assess proposals designed to accommodate those interests. A facilitative-narrow approach helps parties become "realistic" about their situation but does not use the mediator's own assessments, predictions, or proposals to evaluate proposals.

The approach used by a mediator is influenced by his or her past experience, training and ideology as well as the context in which mediation takes place. When mediators describe their work as "an art not a science", they are referring to their role in the process. This focus on role-taking suggests that mediation approaches are dependent upon the mediator's perspective of his or her part in the process as well as their perspective of the other players. A mediator's perspective informs his or her choice about the order and use of particular tactics for the resolution process at hand (Kolb, 1983).

Benefits of Mediation

• • • • • • • • • • • • •

Mediation is more likely to get to the root cause of the problem and thus have a more lasting impact.

A number of benefits have been attributed to mediation. For one, it is voluntary, meaning that parties can leave the table if they so chose. For another, mediation is generally less expensive than litigation, more expedient and convenient in that sessions can be scheduled at times suitable for both parties. Mediation is considered a better process than litigation given the frequent inability of the adversarial process to produce a satisfactorily adequate solution to interpersonal problems. For example, many cases before the courts involve people who know each other or who are involved in ongoing interaction. By the time disputes between neighbours, relatives or landlords and tenants reach the courts, there are often long and complex histories of disagreements and interpersonal tension. The courts provide little opportunity for thorough examination of the problems encountered by the parties and can rule only upon the legal merits of the case. Often this is not the most important issue, and even though one side "wins" in court, both parties are often dissatisfied with the outcome. Instead of polarizing parties, mediation encourages parties to focus on the problem and helps them to achieve mutual understanding and satisfactory outcomes in the resolution of their differences. Mediation is more likely to get to the root cause of the problem and thus have a more lasting impact.

Parties are generally more satisfied with solutions that are mutually agreed upon than those imposed by a third party, therefore compliance is high. In a study by Cook, Roehl and Sheppard (1980), eighty to ninety percent of disputants in varied criminal and civil disputes were satisfied with the mediator, the terms of the agreement, and the mediation process. Similar findings have been found in other studies[7]. One of the more striking findings is that favorable attitudes toward mediation stem largely from how the process works, not from the outcome of the process. Two features are responsible for this: the degree of participation in the decision making that the parties experience, and the fuller the opportunity to express themselves and communicate their views (Bush, 1996).

• • • • • • • • • • • • •
[7] See, Davis, Tichane, and Grayson, "Mediation and Arbitration as Alternatives to Prosecution in Felon Arrest Cases: An Evaluation of the Brooklyn Dispute Resolution Centre", 1980; McEwen, and Mainman, "Small Claims Mediation in Maine: An Empirical Assessment," 1981; Kressesl, Pruitt, and Associates, *Mediation Research.* 1989

Mediation goes beyond
the "quick fix" to become
an opportunity to
strengthen relationships
by fostering mutual
recognition and gain.

For many, the attraction of mediation is much more than utilitarian. It is a vehicle for empowering individuals and groups to manage their own disputes without recourse to professionals or formal institutions. It allows them to regain control of their lives and achieve greater access to justice. Mediation goes beyond the "quick fix" to become an opportunity to strengthen relationships by fostering mutual recognition and gain. For others, mediation promises a new form of community and justice. It holds the potential to transform society.

The Training of Mediators

There is much concern about the education and training of mediators. Some think that mediation is a new profession requiring academic credentials, while others argue that lay personnel should not be precluded from practicing as mediators. Related to this concern is whether a set number of hours of skill-based courses are sufficient to practice or whether a more systematic course of study which includes theory is required. This has resulted in a diversity of training approaches ranging from intensive day long courses to doctorate level programs.

A significant increase in the number of course offerings is to be found in Canadian colleges and universities. Students now learn about effective management and resolution of conflict in business, public administration, criminology, law, education, human and social development, nursing, psychology and social work. In the last year or so, graduate level programs have come to the fore in a number of universities including Carleton, Toronto, York, Victoria, and Royal Roads. Widespread growth has also occurred on American campuses. During the past decade, the number of schools of business and management offering dispute resolution classes has grown from zero to over 200, and of the 175 American accredited law schools more than 150 offer ADR courses compared to only 25 in 1980 (Crohn, 1992). Two of the more noted programs are Harvard Law School's Program on Negotiation, and George Mason University's doctorate degree in conflict resolution. The Consortium on Peace Research, Education, and Development (COPRED) supports an integrated theoretician-practitioner model. COPRED's members, in addition to thirty-two colleges and universities in the United States, include the Universities of Waterloo (Canada), Haifa (Israel), and Bradford (England). The U.S. Academy of Peace and Conflict Resolution and the U.N. University for Peace both place emphasis on research, education and public information. The hallmark of all these courses and programs is the utilization of both theory and skill development, a unique combination in academic approaches.

Most mediators are being trained by other practitioners and leaders in the field, and not by academic institutions.

In reality, most mediators are being trained by other practitioners and leaders in the field, and not by academic institutions. This has resulted in an ever increasing number of mediation skill-focused training programs. Course offerings have become less sporadic although they still vary considerably in content, length, and style. This raises some concern about quality. While such training is not standardized, it does appear to be ideational and centres around specific principles, concepts and ideals. Because of the limits of introductory level training and the lack of on-going training and skill evaluation, the mediation community encourages the use of "apprentice" practitioners working with more experienced ones. This technique, known as mentoring, has become an accepted and important method of training especially since knowledge and technique vary by the nature of the dispute and institutional setting. In general, skill based courses should ground "would-be" mediators in a process model, should develop communication skills to help parties feel heard and understood, should provide an understanding of conflict and conflict styles, should teach a range of methods for eliciting underlying interests including the management of a caucus, should develop skills in agreement writing, and finally, should establish an understanding of cross-cultural issues, ethical considerations and limits of mediation.

Mediation Associations

Professional associations play a significant role as a support base for mediators and contribute to their professional development by informing them of trends and issues, new books, training courses, and conferences.

Professional associations play a significant role as a support base for mediators and contribute to their professional development by informing them of trends and issues, new books, training courses, and conferences. There are a number of dispute resolution associations in Canada and the United States, each tending to focus on a distinct area of dispute resolution, and each offering an array of services and resources which include newsletters, conferences, and membership lists as well networking functions and professional seminars. Family Mediation Canada (FMC), a national body established in 1984, is focused on custody and divorce mediation. Its American counterpart, the Academy of Family Mediators (AFM), was created in 1981; both countries have provincial, state and local family mediation associations. AFM sponsors the journal *Mediation Quarterly* which is published to advance professional understanding of mediation from an interpersonal perspective. The Society for Professionals in Dispute Resolution (SPIDR), an American national association established in 1973, promotes the peaceful resolution of disputes and attracts corporate, labour, business and legal dispute resolution specialists and researchers. Both the Canadian (CBA) and American Bar Associations (ABA) have ADR standing committees. The Network: Interaction for Conflict Resolution (Network), a Canadian national organization housed at Conrad Grebel College in Waterloo, Ontario, networks with those interested in alternate dispute resolution dealing with community, criminal justice, school and multicultural disputes, as well as those interested in public policy and environmental issues. The Network hosts a bi-annual conference which brings together academics and practitioners to share the growing body of knowledge and discuss emerging issues. In the off-year, a similar conference is held in the United States by the National Conference on Peacemaking and Conflict Resolution (NCPCR). One other Canadian organization is the Arbitration and Mediation Institute of Canada (AMIC). Other American associations include: the Consortium of Peace Research, Education and Development (COPRED), the National Institute for Dispute Resolution (NIDR), the International Peace Science Society and the International Peace Research Association.

Current Debates and Trends

Given that different mediation models populate the ADR landscape and a diverse professional mix of mediation practitioners occupy the field, it should not be surprising that many fundamental questions about mediation abound. Is it an art or a science? Is mediation settlement-driven or transformative? What roles do mediators play? Should mediators be regulated? These ideological and policy-related questions occupy the mediation community with debates about the right, wrong, and best model of practice. Once such debates took place within a shared understanding of the nature of mediation (Kolb, 1994); today it seems that "mediation is to a great extent what a mediator does" (Wall and Lynn 1993:186).

Mediators ground their approach to mediation in ideological views of what should happen and why. Two ideologies currently dominate the discourse of mediation – individualistic and relational. The individualist framework, according to Bush and Folger (1994), sees the world as made up of separate beings of equal worth but different needs who naturally seek satisfaction of their individual desires. This framework tends to produce a settlement or problem-solving approach. A relational framework views the world as made up of persons with individual consciousness and diverse needs but who are also inherently connected to each other.

Attempts to bring order to the ambiguity of what constitutes mediation have given rise to conflicting views on whether a mediator is a "passive facilitator" or an "active shaper of solutions".

Attempts to bring order to the ambiguity of what constitutes mediation have given rise to conflicting views on whether a mediator is a "passive facilitator" or an "active shaper of solutions". Conflicting goals, visions and practices have led to two major tensions within the mediation community. The first tension is ideological and positions mediation as being either a transformative social justice event or a pragmatic problem-solving process. The second tension is pragmatic and positions mediation as being either a grass-roots social movement or a professional activity. There is little doubt, that as the mediation community moves toward the millennium, debates about which ideology of mediation will assert primacy in the field will escalate.

That conversations about mediation suffer from ambiguity is also not that surprising given that individuals engaged in conflict resolution come from diverse economic, social and political backgrounds. In contrast to the 1970's when many mediators experienced isolation in their work, today's practitioners are found in most sectors of Canadian society. This change in demographics was evident in a recent survey carried out by The Network: Interaction for Conflict Resolution[8]. Not only did their study show a substantive growth in the numbers of mediators, it also showed a shift in membership from community-based volunteer groups to more business oriented individuals in private practice.

The perception of mediation as an emerging profession and growth industry (Picard, 1994) raises serious questions about standards, ethics and certification. While there is universal desire for high quality dispute resolution, there is also concern that legislating who can and cannot practice will unduly curtail the development of the field. At first glance it might appear that having stated policies on standards of conduct is progressive and reflective of mediation as a maturing profession, however this presumes the existence of homogenous ethical values. Canada is a rapidly changing and multi-cultural society, and as the mediation community begins to define what is or is not mediation, this begins a debate that can privilege certain sets of social values.

[8] A summary of the survey findings was printed in the Network's newsletter, *Interaction* Vol. 9 No. Fall 1997

• • • • • • • • • • • •

The field, therefore needs to develop a discourse that more adequately reflects both the approach and ideology of the service being provided.

Referring to a myriad of non-adjudicative dispute resolution processes as "mediation" gives the impression that mediation is a homogeneous event. It is not. The field, therefore needs to develop a discourse that more adequately reflects both the approach and ideology of the service being provided. Doing so will protect the integrity of mediation, as well as ensure that its vitality and growth are not inadvertently restricted. For example, mandatory mediation might be more appropriately labeled a settlement conference, and judge-mediators might disclose that they use "muscle mediation" to enable parties to reach settlement in short time frames. Community mediation programs might publicize their commitment to beliefs rooted in social justice, empowerment and self-determination. Family and divorce mediators might articulate the values surrounding the way in which they practice, for example whether they are directive and evaluative or relational and facilitative; whether they use a feminist-informed model of mediation or a therapeutic-interventionist approach. Creating a distinct discourse that sets out the limits of mediation will make more explicit the value-based and ethical viewpoints of individual mediators.

That mediation encompasses a variety approaches makes is appealing; it also gives cause for criticism. For example, feminist scholars argue that in some circumstances, mediation serves to further oppress women and marginal groups by reinforcing patriarchal and middle-class values. Legal critics contend that mediation produces "second-class justice", marginalizes crime and extends state control. Many of the virtues once attributed to mediation have become myths – claims about neutrality, autonomy, non-cohesiveness, and social justice (Merry, 1989). Whereas in the past, mediation was associated with a discourse of empowerment and transformation; today's benchmarks increasingly speak of cost-effectiveness, timeliness, and satisfaction.

Accommodating cultural
difference is one of the
more challenging issues
facing mediators in
the late 1990's.

Accommodating cultural difference is one of the more challenging issues facing mediators in the late 1990's. It is even more challenging as the field moves toward standardization and regulation, and as more jurisdictions mandate parties to attend mediation. Defining what mediation is or is not requires privileging a particular set of ideological views which ultimately results in legitimizing the dominant culture's values at the expense of other ethnocultural ideologies. In addition, standardization restricts the practice of mediation and poses a threat to its diversity at a time when diversity is perhaps needed most. Insisting that people resolve disputes on the basis of values and customs contrary to their own has been found to be more oppressive than empowering. The trend to define mediation as a single entity greatly disfavours those who are not of the white Western tradition (LeBaron, 1997). Researchers and practitioners must work in close collaboration if mediation is to fulfill its potential as a means to provide more just and humane ways of responding to conflict.

Perhaps one of the most pressing needs of the mediation community is in the area of research. Despite its increasing popularity and use, research on the topic remains relatively sparse. Very few studies on mediation have been carried out in Canada. The studies that have been conducted have, for the most part, focused on who is involved in dispute resolution activities (Department of Justice, 1995), on rates of compliance (Umbreit, 1995), and on levels of satisfaction (Mcfarlane, 1995). Many agree that our understanding of third party procedures is in its infancy. Contemporary mediation can be likened to our knowledge of surgery in the early eighteenth century; training is often by apprenticeship, practice is principally intuitive, and the literature is largely prescriptive. To understand the potential of mediation in Canadian society requires that we systematically assess the value of mediation, its social and political implications, as well as its impact on our quality of life and its potential as a vehicle for social change.

• • • • • • • • • • •

Today's mediators must be reflective...they must take a broad perspective in attempting to understand the dynamics of conflict and the impact of using mediation to resolve social and legal conflict ...they need to utilize holistic and elicitive approaches in their work.

Lack of a sound understanding of this fast growing social phenomenon has implications for those who work in the field; it also has implications for how Canadians respond to conflict on the eve of the 21st century in a post-industrial, "high tech" and multi-cultural world. Already early visions of social transformation are being displaced by case management goals as programs become directed toward meeting the needs of the state and less so to the parties in dispute or to the structural causes of conflict arising from issues of class, ethnicity, gender and culture. It seems that while mediation is expanding, at the same time a common understanding of what constitutes mediation is weakening. Today's mediators must be reflective and be able to think "outside the box". They must take a broad perspective in attempting to understand the dynamics of conflict and the impact of using mediation to resolve social and legal conflict. Finally, they need to utilize holistic and elicitive approaches in their work. The future for mediation in Canada looks promising. It's growth is likely to intensify, its study diversify, and its value multiply. However, to realize the full potential of mediation requires that there be more and easier opportunities for cross-fertilization of ideas and practices. This will enable the richness of mediation to be enthusiastically embraced, and allow mediation to realize its potential as a "real alternative" to other dispute resolution processes. The goal is for mediation to become the primary dispute resolution process, not an alternative.

2

The Practice

Chapter 3:

Conflict

Conflict is something that many people try to avoid or respond to with a "knee-jerk" reaction. Both of these responses result in negative emotions, ineffective solutions and unresolved issues. Conflict theory is based on the premise that conflict can be constructive and healthy. It can improve group cohesiveness, stimulate innovations, and encourage the search for better solutions.

Understanding Conflict

• • • • • • • • • • • •

Conflict, if constructively managed, can contribute to the well-being of individuals and groups.

Conflict is a fact of life. We see examples of it every day ranging from minor disagreements between individuals to political disagreements that have escalated into war. Conflict can also be a mental struggle within ourselves generated from personal needs, desires, temptations, or from our needs and values coming into opposition with those of others.

If conflict is handled badly, it can lead to mistrust, anxiety and dissatisfaction with oneself and with others.

A central concept in conflict management is that conflict does not have to be destructive or dysfunctional. In fact, conflict is healthy and can be productive. Poorly managed conflicts can destroy relationships, families and communities. If managed skillfully and creatively, conflict can bring increased benefits for everyone. It can stimulate interest, improve communication, increase productivity and bring about social change.

Conflict can be useful in bringing about positive change and growth in individuals, organizations and communities. In fact, suppressing conflict can be more costly than conflict itself. To take away conflict is to take away the incentive to grow and learn. Constructive conflict resolution processes promote "win-win" problem-solving.

The ability to resolve conflict is one of the most important social skills individuals can acquire, yet there are few opportunities to learn how to use conflict in positive ways.

We use different ways to resolve conflicts, depending on the situation and the persons involved. For example, you probably do not talk to your boss in the same way that you talk to a friend.

Not only is it important to recognize how we respond to conflict situations, it is also helpful to be aware of our inner reaction. What feelings are evoked? Do we view conflict as an opportunity for learning or is it something we dread and fear? Knowledge of our own reactions to conflict is a first step to making positive change in our lives.

Key Points About Conflict

- In itself, conflict is neither bad nor good. It is good when handled well, bad when not handled well.

- Conflict will always be a part of our lives so we should learn how to manage it creatively and constructively.

- We can all learn conflict management skills to solve our problems.

- Conflict occurs within relationships, individuals, groups, and between groups.

- Conflict is constructive when resolved in ways that enhance relations, destructive when relationships are harmed.

- Conflict is cumulative, so it is important to deal with conflict as it arises.

- A conflict usually develops over time with some incident triggering it to come out into the open.

- We do not always create conflict, but we can always choose our response to it.

Four A's of Conflict Management

Awareness

Acceptance

Analysis

Appropriate Action

Causes of Conflict

Conflicts can originate from many sources which makes it difficult to determine its cause. For constructive conflict resolution, it is important to find the root of a problem. To begin, accept the conflict at face value, then adjust your opinions as you begin to define it. There are three common causes of conflict: competition for limited resources, basic human needs, and values and beliefs.

Competition for Limited Resources

Many conflicts stem from competition over limited resources (money, space, land, jobs). For the most part, these types of conflict tend to be the easiest to resolve. Time, however, plays a critical role. Conflict increases as parties perceive resources to be shrinking.

Basic Human Needs

Needs such as power, success, recognition, friendship, affiliation and self-worth often place us in conflict with others with similar needs. If such conflicts also entail competition for limited resources, the degree of conflict is even greater. Conflicts which involve human needs are more difficult to resolve than conflicts over resources because the reasons for the former are usually less clear and because they are a part of our identity.

Values & Beliefs

Value conflicts include personal priorities as well as religious, cultural and political beliefs. Beliefs and values are of such importance that when they clash the ensuing conflict is often very difficult to resolve. When our values are challenged, we may feel that our whole sense of self is threatened, making us cling to our positions all the more strongly.

In value conflicts, "right and wrong" is not always relevant. Values make perfect sense to the person holding them. When we project our values onto another person or assume that we can motivate them with the same values that motivate us, conflict often arises. Resolving this type of conflict is difficult, especially when those involved value their goals highly. Values-based conflict resolution is best focussed on achieving mutual understanding.

Other Underlying Causes of Conflict

- Self

- Needs or Wants

- Values

- Perceptions

- Assumptions

- Knowledge

- Expectations

- Race and Gender Differences

- Ability and Willingness to Learn from Conflict

Types of Conflict

Intrapersonal
Intrapersonal conflicts are debates that occur within ourselves. They often involve questions related to moral decisions, use of resources, and personal goals.

Interpersonal
Interpersonal conflicts occur between two or more people.

Intragroup
Intragroup conflicts are those that occur between individuals or sub-groups within the same group.

Intergroup
Intergroup conflicts occur between groups (communities, organizations, cultures, nations). One of the problems in dealing with these disputes, whether at the community or international level, is the difficulty in identifying and addressing the myriad of needs, values and concerns expressed by the groups and their members.

Escalation and De-Escalation

Our response to conflict can cause it to escalate or de-escalate.

It will be likely to escalate when:

- other people become involved or take sides
- one party feels threatened by the other
- there is no interest or investment in maintaining a relationship or there is a history of negative conflict
- there is an increase in the indirect expression of anger, fear or frustration
- needs are not acknowledged or met
- people lack the skills to resolve the conflict.

A conflict will be likely to de-escalate when:

- those involved focus on the problem rather than on each other
- emotions of anger, fear and frustration are spoken directly rather than demonstrated indirectly
- threats are reduced or eliminated
- those involved have cooperated well prior to the dispute
- needs are openly discussed
- those involved use conflict management skills or receive help in applying them.

Levels of Conflict

Problem solving.
Disagree, but share problem.

Shift from disagreement
to personal antagonism.

Person seen as problem.

Issue Proliferation.
Specific to general.

Triangle.
Talk about but not with.

Eye for an Eye.
Reaction and Escalation.

Antagonism to Hostility.

Polarization.
Change in social structure.

The Influence of Perception

In conflict, it is wise not to assume that you understand the other person or that the other person understands you.

There are at least two different points of view to any event and, in conflict situations, perceptual limitations have a great impact. Even when speaking the same language we misunderstand because we cannot see into the other's mind or heart.

Although we know that all people are different, we often talk and listen to one another as if we were the same. Our perception of a given situation is influenced by the fact that we come from different families; have different ethnic backgrounds; view conflict through different lenses; have had different personal experiences; want different things from life and from each other; and have different dreams, wishes and expectations. These factors lead us to act differently from others in similar situations.

The relative importance of an issue does not necessarily determine the seriousness of a dispute. Seemingly minor conflicts can escalate into violent confrontations. Our perception of what is "at stake" determines the intensity of the dispute.

Conflict Styles

People, groups and organizations manage conflict in a variety and combination of styles. The utility of each style depends upon the context and the issue, as well as the relationaship we have with the other party. Most of us use each of the five styles described below at one time or another. (Each of the styles are ideal types and are not representative of actual people.) We do, however, tend to have a dominant style or "knee-jerk" reaction.

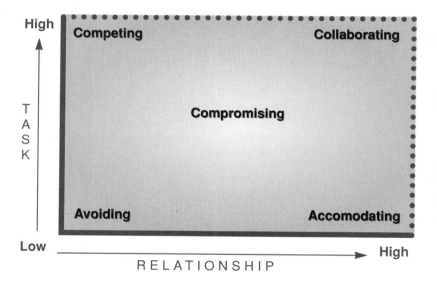

Styles of conflict are built around two factors that are present in every conflict:

i) the goals each party is trying to achieve (assertiveness), and

ii) the relationship the parties have with each other (cooperativeness).

The style we choose is largely determined by the concern we have for one or the other of the above two factors. The five styles are as follows:

Accommodate

When people accommodate, they smooth over situations and want others to like and accept them. They are quick to accommodate others and ignore their own needs because they believe asking others to meet their needs will harm the relationship. The accommodator has a high concern for relationships, is willing to give up personal goals and is often afraid that conflict will damage relations.

Compete

People who compete try to force others to accept their way. They are oblivious to the needs or feelings of others; believe conflicts are settled by one person winning and the other losing. They want to win and will fight at any cost to do so. Those who choose to compete have a high concern for personal goals and a low concern for relationships.

Avoid

When people avoid, they withdraw because they believe it is hopeless to try to resolve conflict. They avoid people and issues that may cause conflict, and they feel helpless to attain goals. Those whose tendancy is to avoid, often assume they cannot achieve their goals or maintain relationships, so decide it is best to withdraw and avoid.

Compromise

People who compromise will give up some goals if others are willing to give up some too. They are less optimistic about conflict bringing improved relationships than those who collaborate. They assume that we cannot get everything we want in a conflict (better to "give a little and get a little"). Compromisers push for some goals, but try not to jeopardize relationships; they allow the other party to get some of what they want.

Collaborate

Those who collaborate confront openly and fairly. They are optimistic about conflict and committed to personal goals and to others' goals. They begin by openly identifying the wishes of both sides and are not satisfied until a solution that is mutually beneficial is found. They combine a high concern for goals and relationships; they assume both parties can achieve their goals and they work toward that end.

Assessing Conflict Guide

This guide is designed to help third party neutrals, as well as disputing parties, examine a conflict situation. It can be used in informal conversation, interviews, or in joint session. The guide is useful when preparing for an intake and as a reflective tool during mediation.

The guide may also be given to parties to help them prepare for mediation

Remember, all conflicts change over time. At best, this guide helps to generate a perspective, not answers. It may need to be adapted for your particular purpose or situation.

Attitudes and Values

- What attitudes toward conflict do parties hold?

- What is the cultural background of the parties, and what is the cultural context in which the conflict takes place?

- How might culture, gender, class, power, personal traits, expectations and perception be operating in this conflict?

Nature of the Conflict

- What "triggered" this conflict to come into the open?

- What is the history?

- Who are the parties – primary and secondary?

- What is the relationship between the parties?

- What are the perceived incompatible goals and scarce resources?

- What values, needs or beliefs are motivating the conflict?

- What interests are in common?

- How does trust factor into the conflict?

Positions and Interests

- What are each parties substantive, procedural and psychological interests?

- What motivates these interests?

- How are interests being framed into positions?

- What are each parties CHEAP BFV's (concerns, hopes, expectations, assumptions, priorities, beliefs, values and fears?)

Power

- What power currencies do the parties see themselves and the other possessing?
- What evidence of destructive power occurs?
- How does power shift? How might it be balanced?
- What unused sources of power are present?

Styles and Tactics

- What negotiation styles are the parties using?
- How do individual styles change during the course of the negotiations?
- How destructive is the tone of this conflict?
- How does anger play itself out and how might it be managed more productively?

Attempted Solutions

- What changes do the parties expect?
- What options have been explored?
- Have attempted solutions become part of the problem?
- Is this a repetitive conflict? If so, what is the overall pattern?
- What categories of attempted solutions have not been tried?

Consensus

To reach consensus requires respect for all ideas, opinions and suggestions.

It requires that we understand all points of view: remember, understanding does not mean agreement.

Consensus is reached when we can understand and accept all points of view before making a decision.

Guidelines for Reaching Consensus

Avoid arguing over rank and position – seriously consider all points of view.

Avoid "win-lose" stalemates – when an impasse occurs search for the next most acceptable solution.

Avoid changing of minds as a way to avoid conflict or achieve harmony.

Avoid majority voting, averaging, bargaining, or coin flipping.

Keep the attitude that different points of view are natural and healthy to a group.

Treat differences of opinion as the result of incomplete sharing of relevant information – keep probing.

When You are Involved in the Conflict

The following points are suggested for use when you are involved in a conflict situation and when handling a verbal exchange.

- Avoid getting angry and be willing to express your feelings

- Keep it simple... use the "ten words or less" rule.

- Encourage and make positive statements.

- Speak clearly and distinctly.

- Try to surface "hidden" hostility. Talk about and attempt to understand the underlying the cause of the conflict.

- Be transparent.

- Listen and restate in your words what you perceive the other is saying. Do not make assumptions.

- Deal with issues, not personalities.

- Avoid the "silent treatment".

- Avoid bringing up past behaviours that have nothing to do with the current situation.

- Accept honest feedback.

- Strive for a win/win situation.

Reducing Defensiveness

Once again, when you are involved in the conflict, the following "tips" should prove helpful.

> ☒ *Don't Evaluate...*
> ☑ Describe

People become defensive when they are labeled or called names. Describe behaviour rather than evaluating it.

> ☒ *Don't Corner the Other...*
> ☑ Help to Save Face

People become defensive when put in a corner with no way to save face. Suggest possibilities, explore options and brainstorm solutions.

> ☒ *Don't be Superior...*
> ☑ Promote Equality

Try not to come across as superior, you are in this together.

> ☒ *Don't Focus on Control...*
> ☑ Focus on the Problem

Rather than telling what should be done, work to problem-solve collaboratively.

> ☒ *Don't Appear Neutral...*
> ☑ Show Your Empathy

Instead of hiding feelings to appear neutral, show empathy. Neutrality can appear uncaring, standoffish or hostile.

> ☒ *Don't Manipulate...*
> ☑ Share Solution

If feeling manipulated, people are less likely to cooperate.

> ☒ *Don't Be So Certain...*
> ☑ Be Provisional

Let go of having to be "right". Communicate willingness to change your behaviour and ideas – use provisional language.

Chapter 4:

Communication

Listening is a very
important skill for
mediators and accounts
for well over 90%
of time spent in a
mediation session.

It is said that humankind's most significant achievement is communication. As a result of advanced technology, we can communicate with people on the other side of the country, the world and even the moon. Yet, face to face, we often have difficulty saying what really matters – personal feelings that reveal who we really are and what we actually feel. It is also difficult to listen to what another person is saying and to really understand them.

Good communication is essential for the management of conflicts. Each person must be heard and understood and feel heard and understood in order for there to be a lasting resolution. The main task of a mediator is not to get parties to communicate (they already have been), but rather to help them communicate in a way that ensures they both hear and understand one another.

To understand, we must uncover emotion and factual content. Words alone can be misleading.

Communication Process

Communication is a process where messages are sent and received from one person to another. Messages contain two parts – factual content and personal emotion. Words can be heard and actions seen, but we can only infer what these words and actions mean. Most of us keep our emotions and thoughts private and hidden, however, clues to feelings can be found in behaviours if we probe to uncover them.

A good listener pays attention to what is said and to how it is said. They watch for the non-verbal message and read "between the lines" to seek support for, or contradictions to, the verbal message.

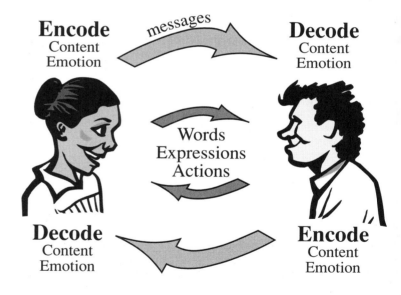

Encode
Content
Emotion

messages

Decode
Content
Emotion

Words
Expressions
Actions

Decode
Content
Emotion

Encode
Content
Emotion

Communication Breakdown

A break-down in communication can occur for a variety of reasons.

- A speaker's thoughts and feelings are known only to him/her so the listener has to guess at what they are. The listener's interpretation is also private, so neither party may be aware that a misunderstanding exists.

- It is believed that 75% of oral communication is ignored, misunderstood and quickly forgotten.

- Words often have different meanings for people, particularly if they are from different cultures or groups.

- People talk about the presenting problem when the underlying problem is of more concern.

- It is often difficult to discuss the things that are most important to us. Consequently, we come up with solutions to minor problems, but do not address deeper concerns.

- Speakers may be unaware of their emotions. We are taught to repress feelings (boys don't cry; nice girls don't get angry) and this can control our actions.

- Listeners are distracted by thoughts or events around them. They hear through filters developed from experience and prejudice which may distort what is said. We often hear what we expect others to say.

- We can think at 400-500 words per minute but only speak at 125-150 (which leaves us with a lot of time to "tune out").

Non-Verbal Communication

A good listener pays attention to what is said and to how it is said. They watch for the non-verbal messages and read "between the lines" to support or contradict the verbal message. Most non-verbal communication deals with feelings which are more powerful than the rational or factual part of a message.

Non-verbal expression includes body movement, posture, eye contact, facial expression, gestures and physical distance. When a verbal message and a non-verbal message conflict, we usually defer to the non-verbal message as the truth. Remember the adage "actions speak louder than words".

Tone, volume and clarity of voice are also considered cues to underlying messages. These are indirect verbal cues.

The truth is that you cannot "not communicate". Your smile, frown, posture and gestures reveal how you are feeling. It is estimated that well over half of what we communicate is by way of non-verbal messages. To illustrate this point:

- 55% of what is communicated comes from body movement and facial expressions

- 38% comes by way of voice tone, volume and clarity

- 7% comes from words alone.

Voice Tone, Volume and Clarity 38%

Verbal Expression 7%

Body Movement, Facial Expressions 55%

Barriers to Communication

Criticizing:
Focusing on the negative aspects of the situation induces guilt and lowers self-esteem. *"You never think of anyone but yourself when you make decisions!"*

Praising to Manipulate:
Using praise as a gimmick to try to get people to change their behaviour or for ulterior motives. Praise can be used to control or manipulate causing people to become guarded and defensive. It implies the ability to judge and establishes a judge/ supplicant relationship. *"There is no doubt that you are smart, and I know if you worked harder you could raise your grades."*

Diagnosing:
Playing emotional detective and probing for hidden agendas arouses anger, rejects, threatens or undermines self-trust. *"You only feel that way because they didn't include you in the final decision-making process."*

Name-Calling and Sarcasm:
Belittling the person by referring to them in the negative creates feelings of resentment and frustration. *"I don't suppose you ever lose your cool under pressure!"*

Ordering:
Forcefully telling a person what to do implies that the other's judgment is unsound and undermines self-esteem. *"You must accept the decision and get on with your life."*

Threatening:
Giving the person an ultimatum for change emphasizes punishment. *"If you don't take my offer, I'll see you in court!"*

Moralizing:
Backing your solution with social, religious or moral authority. *"Any decent moral person would see that I am right on this issue."*

Irrelevant Questions:
Questions that are incomplete, impersonal or veiled imply distrust and cause defensive reactions and resistance. *"Whatever made you think I would agree with you?"*

Diverting:
Showing lack of respect by diverting the focus of attention to you. *"You think you have it bad; let me tell you about the time that I was asked to lead the team."*

Advising:
Telling the person how you think they should solve the situation implies a lack of confidence in the other person to problem solve and cope with their own problems. Encourages dependency or "yes, but's". *"I think you should refuse his offer and then take him to court".*

Logical Argument:
Focussing on the factual aspects of the conflict while ignoring the emotions of the person can be infuriating when the other person is under stress because the focus is on facts rather than feelings. *"You are wrong! According to this report, you have no reason to believe him or worry about his reaction."*

Reassuring:
Trying to smooth things over can be a roadblock if the listener tries to be helpful but does not experience the person's emotions. It is not empathic and may be too optimistic. *"Don't worry about it, I'm sure you will see things differently tomorrow."*

Reflective Listening

Reflective listening
requires you to listen
for the main ideas and
emotions; clarify to be
sure you understand;
then restate what you
heard in your own words.

Reflective or active listening is a skill with which the listener attempts to hear and accurately feedback the content and the feeling of the speaker's message. Reflective listening shows that the listener is trying to understand how it feels to be the speaker and it intuitively says that the speaker is important.

Reflective listening demands more than nodding your head and saying "uh-huh" from time to time. It requires you to understand the person's words and feelings, and to suspend judgment on what was said. Withholding judgment minimizes the chances of a speaker feeling "put-down", builds trust and encourages people to share information.

Reflective listening involves three sub-skills:

i) **attending** – using nonverbal indicators such as leaning forward in an open, accepting, neutral position

ii) **paraphrasing** – repeating in your own words what the person has said and suspending judgment on what was said

iii) **identifying feelings** – reflecting how a person is feeling (which often requires you to first figure out what that is) without appearing negative or judgmental.

Purpose of Reflective Listening
To check understanding not only of the words spoken by the other person but also of their meaning.

- To demonstrate your interest.
- To help people feel understood.
- To let the speaker think about what he or she has said.
- To encourage the speaker to explain fully.
- To check out unintended meanings.

When to Use Reflective Listening

■ Before acting, arguing or criticizing.

■ When a person has strong feelings or wants to talk over a problem.

■ When another person wants to sort out his or her feelings and thoughts about a specific situation.

How to Listen Reflectively

■ Remain neutral, do not take sides, do not put anyone down.

■ Do not agree or disagree with what has been said.

■ Concentrate on what is being said and restate what was said in your words.

■ Respond to non-verbal clues and show understanding through non-verbal responses, for example, tone of voice, facial expressions, gestures, eye contact, posture.

■ Put yourself in the other person's shoes to understand what the person is saying and how he or she feels.

■ Restate the person's most important thoughts and reflect their feelings.

■ Do not interrupt, finish sentences, offer advice or give suggestions. Do not bring up similar feelings or problems from your own experience.

Tools for Reflective Listening

"HEAR YE, HEAR YE"

Tools for Reflective Listening

Encourage
Clarify
Restate
Reflect
Summarize
Validate

Encourage

Encouraging statements convey interest in what the person is saying and encourage them to keep talking. Do not agree or disagree with what is said and use neutral words. *"Please tell me more about what happened?"* Or, *"I would like to hear more about that incident."*

Clarify

Clarification is used to help you understand what has been said. Asking for clarification may help the speaker to explain further. *"I am not sure I understand what you mean by that; it would help if you would elaborate."*

Restate

Restating the basic ideas and facts in your own words, shows that you are listening and hearing what is being said. It allows you to check the speaker's intended meaning with your interpretation. *"You would like him to spend more time with you, especially on weekends."*

Reflect

Reflecting requires that you "mirror" the speaker's feelings. The purpose of reflecting is to show that you understand how the person feels and to help them evaluate their feelings after hearing them expressed by someone else. *"You're annoyed by what she just said."*

Summarize

Summarizing involves restating the major ideas that have been expressed in order to review progress, pull together important ideas and facts and establish a basis for further discussion. Summarizing is a good technique to use when the conversation seems to be going in circles and you want to refocus on key issues. *"Let me see if I can summarize the key issues that have been expressed so far."*

Validate

Validating is used to acknowledge another person and show appreciation for their actions. It involves acknowledging their ideas, efforts and feelings. *"I appreciate your meeting on such short notice. I know this is a busy time for you."*

Some Feeling Words

For many people, it is difficult to find the right word to express their, or other's, emotions. The following list may prove helpful.

abandoned	apprehensive	cold
abused	apologetic	concerned
accepted	arrogant	confident
acknowledged	ashamed	curious
admitted	attacked	deceived
affronted	bashful	demoralized
afraid	betrayed	demure
agitated	blamed	determined
aggressive	blissful	depressed
angry	bored	despised
annoyed	bothered	disappointed
antagonized	cautious	disapproving
anxious	challenges	disbelieving

discontented
disdained
disgruntled
disgusted
dishonored
displeased
dissatisfied
distressed
disturbed
eager
ecstatic
embarrassed
enraged
envious
exasperated
exhausted
excluded
frightened
frustrated
furious
furious
grieving
guilty
happy
harassed
hesitant
horrified
hot
humiliated
hungry
hung over
hurt
hysterical
honored
ill treated
impatient
included
indifferent
idiotic
indignant

innocent
interested
insulted
irked
irresolute
irritated
jealous
joyful
let down
loaded
lonely
loved
love struck
manipulated
meditative
mischievous
miserable
misunderstood
negative
neglected
nervous
obstinate
optimistic
offended
ostracized
outraged
pained
panicked
perplexed
piqued
powerful
powerless
provoked
prudish
put down
puzzled
rebuffed
recognized
regretful
rejected

relieved
resentful
respected
responsible
restless
sad
satisfied
scorned
sexy
sheepish
shocked
skeptical
slighted
smug
snubbed
spurned
stressed
sure
surprised
suspicious
sympathetic
taken advantage of
thoughtful
trapped
troubled
uncertain
undecided
understood
undervalued
uneasy
unhappy
unnerved
unsure
upset
used
vexed
violated
withdrawn
worried
wounded

Asking Questions

Many of us ask questions that are either too broad and unfocused or too narrow and limiting. As a result, we typically get responses that are vague and noncommittal. Probing is a technique which encourages a person to go beyond what they have said to clarify or elaborate. Asking probing questions can help discover areas of mutual interest and maximize the amount of "free information" (information a person is willing to share).

Probing questions are open-ended. This means that they cannot be answered by "yes" or "no". Probing questions will begin with what, when, where, how, who and, to a lesser extent, why. (Asking why may lead people to become defensive.) Open-ended questions elicit information which helps you to explore further and may provide information not otherwise given. When asking probing questions it is important not to introduce bias or imply that some responses are more acceptable than others.

Examples of Probing Questions and Statements

In what way would that be helpful?

It would help if you would expand more fully on that point.

What would make it possible for you to consider that option?

What else can you tell me about the situation?

What would be an example to help illustrate that point?

Please explain what you meant by that.

What is your concern about his offer?

Carried to a logical conclusion, what do you hope to gain?

Tell me more about what happened.

Sometimes the most effective way to indicate your interest in going deeper into the subject is to use short, open questions such as: *Then what? How did you deal with it?*

What now? and gestures or quizzical facial expressions (raised eyebrows, eyes open wide). Learning to ask effective questions takes thought and a good deal of practise. Being able to ask questions effectively will result in an increase in the quality of information you receive.

Silence

Frequently, the best question is silence. All too often we talk to fill an uncomfortable pause in the conversation. Sometimes waiting for the other person to speak (they likely feel just as uncomfortable as you do with the silence) can get you more information than if you ask questions.

Types of Questions

Different types of questions serve different functions.
The way a question is worded will greatly affect the answer
and the willingness of a party to supply information.

- **General** (most open and indirect)

  What is it?

  What is the background to this situation?

  What brought you here?

  How did it happen?

- **Opinion Seeking** (open and directed)

  What do you think about this version of the proposal?

  What would you have done if you were in her place?

  What would satisfy you?

  What would you have liked him to do differently?

- **Fact-Finding** (somewhat open and directed)

  How long will it take to get the money?

  When is it that you need the information?

  Where is the meeting taking place?

  Who else should be involved in making this decision?

- **Narrow or Forced Choice** (mostly closed)

  Can you give him the money by Friday?

  Have you told him about this before?

  Did you actually see it happen?

  Is that your final offer?

- **Leading** (closed)

  If you didn't see him, can you really be sure he took it?

  Is it true that you were present at that meeting?

  If she agrees to your plan, will that satisfy you?

  You really want to believe the student's story, don't you?

Reframing

• • • • • • • • • • •

The ability to see a number of frames of reference for any given problem and to be able to suggest alternative frames is an important skill for anyone wishing to facilitate conflict resolution.

Reframing is the process of changing how a person defines or conceptualizes a particular situation or event. In resolving conflicts, it is important to remember that our perception and emotional response to a particular event is based on the frame of reference within which it is viewed. It is possible to change the meaning of an event by changing this frame of reference. If this happens our attitude and our response to the situation can also change.

Conflict is often caused by individuals seeing a situation from different perspectives. The result of which is a struggle to make the other person see it from your perspective. What we are really asking is for them to change their frame of reference which is usually difficult. Each "framing" of a situation has truth and relevance to the person who holds it.

Reframing extracts the positive or useful content from what was said. It may also suggest an action which would assist parties reach a desirable outcome. It can be used to identify underlying interests, soften demands, modify deadlines, decrease threats, and remove emotional or value-laden language.

Reframing is a rewording technique which puts issues in terms that both parties understand and which leads them in the direction of a "win-win" solution. It is used to:

- Emphasize a positive goal

- Emphasize common ground

- Identify underlying needs

- Eliminate accusations or blaming

- Expand to the fuller meaning of a message.

- Shift positional statements to issue or interest statements

General Procedures for Reframing

- Say it in other words (paraphrase).
- Summarize and condense.
- Put issues into a logical sequence.
- Elaborate on limited information (underlying issues, concerns and feelings).
- Break issues into smaller and more manageable sub-issues.
- State issues in broader terms.
- Remove emotions or value-laden language by stating issues in a non-judgmental or non-emotional way.

Where to Focus When Reframing

- Issues definition
- Positions to interests
- Toxic language
- Complaints to requests
- Individual to joint
- Past to future
- Blame to problems

How to Reframe

Formula:

"It sounds like <u>(value or need)</u> *is important to you.*

OR

"<u>(Value or need)</u> *is something you seem to value a lot."*

Example:

STATEMENT: *"How dare you go into my room and read my diary!*

REFRAMED: *"It sounds like you need me to respect your privacy".*

Other examples of reframed statements:

Example of shifting a position to an issue:

There is no way that I am going to agree to those hours.

REFRAME: *So, one of the things we have to talk about is what time your daughter comes home at night.*

Example of shifting an either/or statement to an issue:

Either you give me what the watch is worth or I'll see you in court.

REFRAME: *One of the issues is the value of the watch.*

Example of shifting a position to an interest:

It was not my fault sthat the window broke, so I refuse to pay you any money.

REFRAME: *You are worried about being blamed for breaking the window.*

Example of shifting from a negative to a positive orientation

I can't stand being at home because my Mom doesn't trust me.

REFRAME: *You are hoping that by coming to this meeting your Mom will begin to trust you more.*

Immediacy

Immediacy is the opportunity to examine what is happening in the moment. Communicating in the "here and now" allows emotions to be dealt with and attended to as they emerge; it can keep conflict from escalating. Immediacy requires that you are sensitive to what is happening beyond the task at hand, and that you share your thoughts and feelings. It requires you to be fully present and take in non-verbal cues between:

- one party and the other

- one or both parties the mediator

- or within the process itself

Immediacy has three requirements: perception, skill and courage. Perception involves taking in both the verbal and non-verbal messages; skills include self-disclosure, feedback and assertion; and courage is required to respectfully state your thought and feelings.

Examples:

> *"You both seem to be feeling pretty hopeless and discouraged about your decision to move,"*

> *"It is clear you both feel strongly about the issues and you're struggling with listening to each other without interrupting."*

> *"Linda, it sounds like you're wondering if I will be helpful to you in settling this."*

> *"Fred, you're looking upset about what I just said. What's going on for you?"*

> *"You seem to be spinning your wheels right now. Is it worthwhile for you to spend more time here, or shall we move on?"*

Bridging

Bridging is a connecting strategy that requires you to link listening and speaking skills. It involves checking out the meaning of the speaker's statement, followed by a probing question or confronting statement designed to lead them to further explore the interests, intent, interpretation or assumptions behind the statement.

Example 1

Empathetic Response

> "John, it is clear that you are expecting Connie to have said or done something, and the look on your face now tells me that you are becoming increasingly impatient that she hasn't."

Bridge

> "It might help the two of you move forward if you could tell us what it is that you are expecting and why it is important to you?"

Bridging is a useful skill to help the mediator move from stage two to stage three and to link various aspects of each person's story.

Example 2

Empathetic Response

> "You went over to show Ann the plans for the addition to your house with the expectation that she would be interested and pleased for you. Instead, and much to your surprise, she became angry and accused you of being inconsiderate."

Bridge

> "It might help if you would explain to Ann why you thought she would be pleased about the addition. Then, it would be helpful if you Ann, would explain why you are not happy about the addition. Sue, let's start with you."

Confrontation

Confrontation is a skill that is used to point out discrepancy related to the issue under discussion or the relationship. When the mediator identifies and then explores these discrepancies, valuable information can resurface. Confronting can help clarify underlying intentions.

The elements of confronting are observing, describing and questioning.

Confrontation points out discrepancies between:

■ What is said at one time and at another.

"Last week you said you were going to see an unemployment counsellor and now it sounds like you've said you decided not to go. What changed for you?"

■ What is done at one time and at another.

"You've been looking for part-time work since January and now you've stopped. How come?"

■ One's goals and the behaviour used to achieve them.

"Michael you've said you were here to resolve your conflict with your Dad over your schooling, yet every time we start talking about it, you begin to talk about your hopes for a summer job. I'm wondering what topic you want to talk about today."

Watch your tone of voice when confronting. Disputants will react defensively if they perceive you to be judging, accusing or blaming. To be effective, confronting should demonstrate curiosity. It should be done with care and sensitivity.

Use sparingly – the skill can be intimidating.

Non-Defensive Responses

Asking an inquiring or clarifying question when confronted by an angry person can help to de-escalate the speaker's emotion. Responding in this way is responding non-defensively. Non-defensive responses aim to break the cycle of "attack and defend" often prevalent in conflict situations. The object is to ask for clarification without becoming defensive.

The following dialogue is an example of non-defensive responses in action.

Attacking statement: *Your attitude is really annoying me.*

Inquiring question: *What is it that I am doing to upset you?*

Attacking statement: *There you go with that "higher than thou" attitude!*

Clarifying statement: *It would help to know what I am doing to annoy you.*

Non-defensive responses help to neutralize a verbal attack because they seldom give the speaker anything further to attack with or defend. However, it often takes a series of clarifying questions and responses before the speaker calms down enough to problem-solve or listen to your point of view. Tone of voice and other non-verbal expressions play a critical role in our success at using non-defensive responses.

Non-blaming Statements

Being able to say how you feel about a situation in a way that does not place blame or accuse is an important conflict resolution skill.

An "I" message is one way of communicating that lowers the level of conflict. A "you" message always raises the level of conflict. "You" messages usually blame, accuse, threaten, order, put-down or make the other person feel guilty and cause them to defend themselves rather than try to solve the problem.

An "I" message tells how you feel, what you want when you feel that way and why you feel that way. It allows you to assert your feelings in a non-threatening way. "I" messages have three parts:

> *I FEEL... (your feelings)*
>
> *WHEN... (behaviour or situation that is a problem)*
>
> *BECAUSE... (the effect of the behaviour on you)*

"I" messages implicitly say... I trust you to care about my feelings and to decide what change in behaviour is necessary.

Example

"You" message:

> *You are always taking my clothes without asking or even telling me; you are not to be trusted!*

"I" message:

> *I get annoyed when my clothes are taken and not returned because when I decide to wear the outfit and it is not there, nothing else ever seems to look right.*

Be careful your "I" message is not really a disguised "you" message. Avoid saying "when you..."

Asking for Feedback

Asking for a person's reaction relieves you of having to guess what they are thinking. The best way for you to do this is to be straight forward (What is your reaction to what I have just said? How do you feel about my saying no? What do you think of her idea?). When you think the message has been received differently than you intended, it is important to check it out. Asking for feedback is a powerful way to avoid misunderstanding. Here are some openers:

She was trying to tell you what it was like; what did you hear her say?

He has told you a lot; what was the message that you heard?

You are frowning; what does that mean?

Your tone of voice leads me to think you are upset; is that true?

DANGER

Check your assumptions
before diving in

Water?

Words to Watch

Some words can be annoying, others more neutral. One of the most challenging tasks is to help people calm down and keep already upset emotions from escalating. A useful skill is to use words as "verbal cushions".

Verbal cushions can let people know that we understand why they may feel a certain way – not that we know exactly how they feel (we are never able to know that). We also want to acknowledge that people have a right to feel the way that they do, and to avoid blaming phrases.

Blaming Phrases	Communication Helpers
I know how you feel.	I understand how you might feel.
You sure are angry.	I can see how you would be angry.
You are not making sense.	I am having trouble understanding your point.
Did you really say that?	Here is what I understood you to say.
You are definitely wrong.	Let me see if I have this straight.
You can't do that.	Let's see if we can find any other solutions.

Point of View Statements

People speak from experience and perception. It is useful to remember that when we speak, it is from our own point of view, and not necessarily the other person's. The other's point of view is just as valid to him or her. When expressing points of view, **describe what happened, don't judge what happened.**

Global Statements

Global statements blame and insult the person instead of pointing out a specific behaviour which may be problematic. Statements such as, *"you always...; you never...; you are..."* lead people to feel defensive.

Culture and Communication

Culture greatly influences the way we communicate. Culture is the system of knowledge shared by a large group of people. Borders between cultures can, but do not usually, coincide with political boundaries between countries. We often hear people refer to American, Japanese or Mexican culture for example. In Canada, we have a number of cultures, some of which include anglophone, francophone and aboriginal to name only a few.

Cultural diversity brings many benefits to our lives including creativity, risk-taking, new perspectives and increased productivity. However, for these advantages to occur, people must understand how they and others communicate. Language may not be the real barrier. Lack of knowledge about the norms and rules guiding communication often is.

Categorizing how people from other cultures and sub-groups communicate is problematic in and of itself – the danger lies in inaccurate and unfavourable stereotyping which may breed racist attitudes. Yet, it is important to learn how to communicate effectively with people from different backgrounds and cultures in order to interpret their messages as they meant them to be interpreted. The spectrum of individualism-collectivism, and high-low context communication styles are helpful in understanding how communication can vary across cultures.

Individualism-Collectivism

Countries such as Canada, the United States and Great Britain have individualist cultures where emphasis is placed on achieving individual goals and self-realization. People are expected to look after themselves and their immediate families. Personal identity is emphasized over social identity when communicating.

In collectivist cultures in Africa, Asia, Japan, China, Central and South America, group goals take precedence over individual ones. Individuals are required to fit into the group – the "we" identity is foremost. In communication, emphasis is placed on the social, rather than the personal, identity.

Individual and collective tendencies exist in all cultures, however, it is likely that one dominates. Thus, these tendencies fall along a continuum. For example, Canadian and American cultures are at the low context end, slightly above are the German, Scandinavian and Swiss cultures; while at the high context end, we find most Asian cultures.

Low/High Context Communication Styles

Cultural differences influence communication. For example, in individualist cultures, information is coded largely in the verbal message. This is a low-context message. Individualist, low context cultures communicate in a direct fashion. Canadians and Americans have a low context communication style.

In collectivist cultures, much of the information to be communicated is encoded in the context or non-verbal expression. Very little is verbally transmitted. This is a high context message. Members of high context, collectivist cultures communicate in an indirect fashion. Many Asian cultures have a high context style of communication.

••••••••
(For further information on individualist/collectivist cultures see William Gudykunst's book *Bridging Differences: Effective Intergroup Communication*. Newbury Park: Sage Publications, 1991).

Chapter 5:
Mediation

• • • • • • • • • • •

Mediation is the inter-
vention of an acceptable
and impartial third party
in a dispute. A mediator
has no decision-making
power and helps parties
reach an agreed upon
solution to the dispute.

As friends, parents, neighbours, or co-workers, it is
not uncommon for us to be called upon to intervene in
disputes involving others. Sometimes we play the role
of arbitrator or decision-maker. There are times, however,
when it may be more useful to help the parties resolve
their own dispute without making decisions for them.
This process is called mediation.

Mediation has, for the most part, been used to resolve
labour, political and organizational disputes. More recently,
mediation has also been used to resolve family, business
and neighbourhood disputes.

Mediation brings people together to talk about their
conflict and accept responsibility by requiring them to
communicate and work together to find their own solution
to the problem. Most importantly, the conflict is solved
jointly.

For mediation to occur, the parties must be willing to talk face-to-face. Communication is often frank. The objective of which is to reach mutual understanding of the situation and recognition of each other's interests. Doing so enables parties to find mutually satisfying resolutions and ones which meet the personal standards of fairness for each party.

A mediator does not take sides, does not judge which party is right or wrong, and does not have any authoritative decision-making power.

The role of the mediator is to try to understand each side in the dispute and make sure the parties understand one another's perspective. An important task is to identify the shared interests, in addition to those they disagree on.

Benefits of Mediation

- accessible, informal and convenient
- structures the negotiation process in ways that lead to increased information becoming available to the parties
- provides the opportunity for parties to express themselves and communicate their views
- provides opportunities for empowerment and growth
- provides a setting in which suspicions and misconceptions can be cleared up
- avoids the win-lose syndrome
- parties are able to participate in decision-making
- solutions can be flexible and tailored to parties needs
- more expedient and less costly than court
- decreases court caseloads and related public expense
- produces high satisfaction and compliance rates
- leads to the restoration of community values
- reduces tension and violence
- brings closure to long standing disputes

Mediation also ...

- ✔ Builds trust and self esteem.
- ✔ Reduces tension and frustration.
- ✔ Unifies people.
- ✔ Promotes self-reliance.
- ✔ Prevents violence and physical abuse.
- ✔ Decreases hostility.
- ✔ Teaches decision making and problem solving.
- ✔ Develops a lifetime skill.
- ✔ Leaves time for doing other things!

The Mediation Process

STAGE ONE
Introduce the Process

STAGE TWO
Identify the Issues

STAGE THREE
Explore the Interests

STAGE FOUR
Generate Solutions

STAGE FIVE
Reach Agreement

STAGE ONE:

Introduce the Process

Welcome the parties and thank them for coming.
Introduce yourself and ask the parties their names if you
do not know them. Give a brief description of the process.

> *Each of you will have ample opportunity to speak.*
>
> *I/We will not judge right or wrong, nor take sides.*
>
> *I/We will help you discuss issues and search for
> solutions you can both agree to. You will decide
> the outcome.*
>
> *If an agreement is reached and if it would be
> helpful, I/we will write out an agreement and give
> each of you a copy.*

If appropriate, clarify each person's authority to settle.
Confirm time limits. Set a positive tone and be encouraging.

Assure the parties that you will keep what is discussed
confidential. Ask how they wish to deal with the issue
of confidentiality. Discuss note-taking.

Explain that mediation will work best if:

- One person speaks while the
  other listens.

- All relevant information is shared.

- You focus on what the situation is like
  for you rather than pointing blame at
  the other person.

Invite questions. Ask each party if they agree to proceed.

STAGE TWO:

Identify the Issues

Request a *brief* (2-3 minutes) opening statement from each side. Ask them why they came to mediation and what they need to discuss. This gives each party a chance to explain the situation and what is important to get resolved. Remember... you are asking each party for a brief overview of the situation in the opening statements. Assure them that you will give them ample opportunity to describe the situation as the mediation progresses.

For example:

> *"Now what I am going to do is ask each of you to make a brief opening statement of 2-3 minutes to get an overview of the situation and find out what each of you were hoping to accomplish here today."*

Ask who wants to begin. If neither party offers, find an impartial way to ask one party to start *(I like to start with the person sitting on my right, so Sam why don't you begin; or, Les, you contacted the Centre, why don't you begin.)*

Restate briefly after each person gives their opening statement to be sure you have understood. Restating also ensures each person has heard the other's perspective.

It may take some time to get at issues, particularly in multi-issue disputes. It is normal to require more than opening statements before all the issues are on the table. Summarize briefly by combining the individual views of both parties as a means of setting an agenda and direction for discussion. This is referred to as an issue statement.

For example:

> *Sam, you lent your notes to Les and they have not been returned. Les, you borrowed the notes and cannot find them. Offering to replace them has not resolved the situation. It seems we need to talk more about the notes, what losing them has been like for each of you, and how to deal with their loss.*

STAGE THREE:

Explore the Interests

This is the heart of mediation; it is where the "magic" occurs. After both parties have made opening statements, use open-ended questions (when, what, where, how) to expand upon the issues presented. Discover underlying interests (feelings, concerns, fears and needs). You are trying to broaden the discussion and uncover emotions. *"How long since this happened? What was your assumption when the notes were not returned? How did you feel when you discovered they were missing? What is important about this for you?"* The objective is to help the parties understand what is important for them, what is motivating them and the other person, and why.

Ask CHEAP BFV (concerns, hopes, expectations, assumptions, priorities, beliefs, fears, values) questions to help uncover the interests and motivating factors giving rise to the conflict.

Prioritize the issues based on potential areas for movement or the perception of importance. Work on identifying other areas of movement. Break larger issues into sub-issues. When there are numerous issues, it help to write them on a flipchart, chalk board or easel. Reframe to identify indirect or negative interests.

Identify what it is that both parties agree upon and what it is that they have in common. Highlight areas of progress.

When appropriate, speak to parties privately (caucus). Work to maintain a climate of rational negotiation by managing personality issues.

Avoid premature assessments. Act as an agent of reality in joint sessions and in caucus. Help parties to focus on objective criteria. Continue to remind parties of their progress, emphasizing areas of agreement and common ground.

After individual and mutual interests have been identified, it is time to form a goal statement. Goal statements should reflect goals, common as well as exclusive interests.

Formula

Given that you both want _____ (goal) _____ , and you both value _____ (mutual interests) _____, how can you come to an agreement that meets your needs, Sue, for _____ (exclusive or complementary interests) _____, and your needs, Ann, for _____ (exclusive or complementary interests) _____?

Common errors when forming a goal statement:

- too general or vague

- positional (does not reflect interests)

- unbalanced (reflects dominance of one party's interests)

- unmanageable (combines too many issues)

There may be times when it is necessary to have several goal statements depending upon the complexity of the situation.

STAGE FOUR:

Generate Solutions

Encourage parties to continue negotiating. Invite them to generate additional options for agreement and closure.

Brainstorm by putting creative energy into thinking of as many solutions as possible to the problem. Do not judge or belittle any ideas. Discourage "bottom lining" and, if appropriate, remind parties of the consequences of not reaching agreement.

If the parties are having difficulty coming up with solutions, you may tentatively make some suggestions. Be careful that they do not feel obligated to accept your suggestions and that they are free to reject them without feeling threatened or forced to lose face. *"What if..."; I'm wondering if you might want to look at...; might it be worth considering..."* Avoid making too many suggestions. It is important that the parties come up with their own solutions. Keep asking for suggestions.

Work together to find a solution acceptable to both parties. This often involves some compromising. Find a way in which both parties can "win" some of what they want.

STAGE FIVE:

Reach Agreement

Congratulate each party. They worked hard to solve their problem. Write out what each side agreed to do, numbering each item. Use full names; specify the terms in as much detail as possible (who, what, where, when, how). Write out dollar amounts. Do not use inflammatory language or imply guilt. Check that the agreement is balanced. Have each party sign the original and give each person a copy to help avoid confusion. In some circumstances, a mediator may want to draft an agreement outside of mediation, to be viewed by parties and their lawyers, then signed at a later date.

A good solution will be:

FAIR
— equitable and satisfactory to both parties

WISE
— specific about when, where, who, and how

EFFICIENT
— realistic so each person can do what they agreed to

STABLE
— agreed to by both parties.

If necessary, suggest other ADR processes if a final agreement cannot be reached.

Moving from Positions to Interests

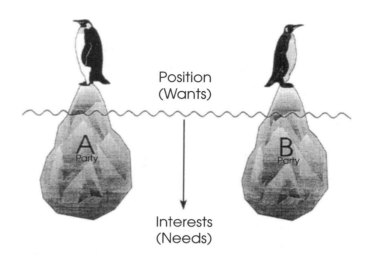

Position
(Wants)

Interests
(Needs)

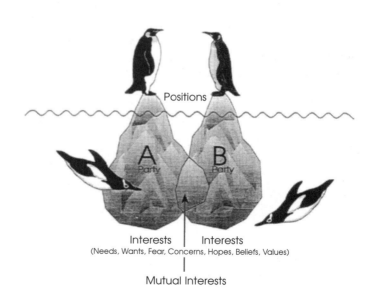

Positions

Interests
(Needs, Wants, Fear, Concerns, Hopes, Beliefs, Values)

Mutual Interests

Positions and Interests

The real problem in conflict situations is not the position (what they want) of each person, but the reasons underlying the position (feelings, needs, fears, concerns). These are "interests" and they are what motivate us. A position is adopted on the basis of interests.

Looking at interests rather than positions makes it possible to find solutions to problems for two reasons:

i) for every concern there exist several possible positions that could satisfy it. Too often we adopt the most obvious position, but if we look behind opposing positions for the motivating interest we can often find an alternative position which meets everyone's needs; and

ii) behind opposed positions lie a range of concerns, many of which are held in common.

We tend to assume that because one person's position is opposed to the other's, their interests are also opposed. In many conflicts, however, an examination of the underlying interests reveal the existence of more concerns that are shared and compatible than are opposed.

One way to think about interests is to think of the formula CHEAP BFVs. Interests are concerns, hopes, expectations, assumptions, priorities, beliefs, fears and values.

How to Identify Interests

Ask Why and Why Not

Put yourself in the other person's shoes and after each position they take, ask yourself why they might be making that demand. Analyze individual consequences of agreeing or refusing the other's position as they might see it.

Look for Multiple Concerns
In most conflicts, people have more than one interest which are influenced by basic human needs (security, recognition, sense of belonging, economic well-being, and control over one's life). Conflicting parties can usually be sensitive to the other party's concerns and needs.

Make a List
To keep clear the various concerns of each party, it often helps to jot down the key points as you hear them. Notetaking also helps place issues in some form of order, and helps keep track of suggestions for solving the situation. Details are less important. Taking too many notes may be more distracting than helpful.

Be Specific
In order for parties to consider interests, they must be identified, understood and legitimized. One way of doing this is to be specific, giving concrete details ("This is the third time that I have heard you say that you asked for input and never got it"). You want to make them think how they might feel if they were in the other's shoes ("How would you feel if someone you cared about appeared to be ignoring you?").

Acknowledge Other's Interests
People listen best when they feel understood – it is important to show that concerns have been heard by restating and reflecting. It is very helpful to acknowledge shared concerns *("It would be unfortunate for both of you if this cannot be resolved as you both have the interests of the group in mind.")*.

Focus on Interests and Be Flexible
Focus on underlying concerns first and positions last. Be flexible and open to new ideas. There may be options that have not been generated which may meet each party's interests. Help the parties to keep an open mind.

Conducting an Intake

What The Parties Needs To Know

- how mediation works
- purpose of mediation
- role of mediator
- who attends
- who is in charge of decision-making
- limits of confidentiality
- time frames
- fees
- value of mediation and consequences of not attending
- recourse if mediation is not successful

What The Mediator Needs to Know

- name and contact information
- who are the stakeholders
- overall nature of dispute but not all the details
- brief history and actions taken to date
- special needs
- safety issues

Assess Suitability

- willingness to participate
- incentives to settle
- competency – physical, emotional
- power relations
- legal, policy or human rights considerations

Assign Tasks

- prepare thoughts on what is to be negotiated
- organize relevant written documents

Collecting Background Information

Data collection and analysis are important skills. They enable a mediator to develop a plan, avoid entering a dispute inappropriately, obtain current information, clarify issues, and identify key people and relationships. The following are some ways to collect and analyze data.

Direct Observation

- attend meetings or briefing sessions
- make a site visit

Secondary Sources

- financial records
- minutes of meetings; government documents; annual reports
- newspapers and magazines

Interviews

- before and during mediation sessions
- decide who to interview and in what sequence
  - party who initiates
  - most powerful / influential / formal / informal power positions
  - who might be offended if not talked to first
  - whose cooperation will induce others to participate
  - who is most likely to talk
- talk to secondary sources before interviewing main parties
- clarify mediation process

Necessity for Pre-Mediation

- access divergence of views
- access communication styles
- determine multiple issues and complexity
- high level hostility or potential for violence
- need for additional information before joint session

Preparing for a Mediation

Once a commitment to mediate has been gained, and it has been deemed appropriate that mediation should take place, a number of factors need to be considered before the mediation takes place.

Participants

Includes the disputing parties. May also involve others affected by the dispute – divorcing couples new partners, children, other stakeholders, an advocate, an interpreter, other professionals such as lawyers, therapists, or accountants, subject experts. May also involve helping groups decide on the selection of spokespersons, and plans for taking agreed upon solutions back to the group for ratification.

Location

Should be accessible for all parties, neutral, private, and comfortable. The meeting location should have separate waiting rooms especially if tensions are high, access to smaller rooms for caucus, access to telephones.

Physical Arrangements

Refers to amount of space required, seating patterns (triangle, circle, panel), shape and size of table (boardroom or parlor style), special accommodations (handicapped), easy access to washrooms. Chairs should be of equal size and height. Also includes details such as Kleenex, extra paper and pens, refreshments (water, tea, coffee, cookies) flip chart, markers, agreement forms.

Selection of Mediator

Includes preference for single or co-mediation or a panel of mediators. Consideration should also be given to who is the most appropriate person to mediate – is there a need for special knowledge or experience? Is a particular mediation approach more favourable? Will they be seen as neutral? Is cultural or ethnic representation a factor? Is this an opportunity to "apprentice" a newly trained mediator?

Time and Cost Factors

Consider how much time will be needed for the first session? Will other sessions likely be needed? Is it possible to hold sessions during working hours or on evenings and weekends? Is there outside pressure to conclude the negotiations by a certain date? How will parties pay for mediation?

Seating Patterns in Mediation

Single-mediation model

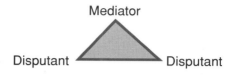

Mediator

Disputant   Disputant

Co-mediation model

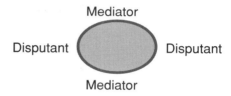

Mediator

Disputant   Disputant

Mediator

Panel mediation model

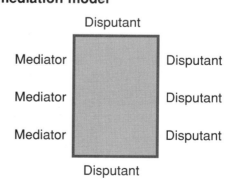

Disputant

Mediator   Disputant

Mediator   Disputant

Mediator   Disputant

Disputant

The Caucus

The caucus is a private meeting held between a mediator and each of the disputing parties. The goal is to uncover resistance to communication between the parties and to promote positive communication and movement towards reaching an agreement.

Purpose of a Caucus

- Allow a breather or cooling off period.
- Check-out each side's perspective.
- Help each side check the reality of their position.
- Encourage the sharing of information.
- Explore new possibilities of movement.
- Discover concerns that have not surfaced in joint session.
- Clarify perceptions and uncover resistance to movement.
- Determine if there are mediator-party issues which should be addressed.
- Suggest ways to promote movement.
- Allow strong feelings to be expressed in private.
- Discuss the mediator's perception to help change views.
- Identify important issues.
- Allow parties to discuss options while not under the scrutiny of the other party.

Calling a Caucus

- Have a specific purpose in mind when calling a caucus.

- Always caucus with both sides.

- Be aware of the length of time spent with each party and be certain that each is not left alone too long.

- Clarify the issue of confidentiality in relation to the information shared in caucus.

- Be certain that you clarify with the parties what is or is not to be kept confidential and take special note of that which is to be kept confidential.

- Maintain an environment of informality and flexibility in the caucus sessions.

- Encourage the parties to seek information and anything else that would assist them to continue negotiating.

During the Caucus

- Keep in mind your original goals, but be flexible in pursuing new ideas and allow for creative problem-solving.

- Keep the responsibility for problem-solving on the parties; resist efforts to have it thrust on you.

- Emphasize strengths – caucusing allows for positive feedback, joint sessions may not.

- Maintain the delicate balance between working to build trust and continuing to communicate your impartiality.

- Be clear what information parties want kept confidential in the joint session.

After the Caucus

- How you re-open the joint session after a caucus is important. Choose the best approach given the information, proposals and feelings which have been shared.

- Be discriminating about what information you share in the joint session. It can facilitate or jeopardize the session. Judgement, timing and respect for privacy are crucial factors.

Writing Agreements

At the Beginning

- Determine what is being achieved today, and whether there can be a final agreement which will be signed by the parties

- Is the agreement to be a draft that requires ratification? If so, by whom and by when?

During the Session

- Take notes.

- Make lists, develop options, and record them.

- Keep the jointly-developed information in front of people.

As an Agreement Takes Shape

- Note key elements.

- Get details, clarification and specifics.

- List all of the commitments and steps to be taken.

Drafting the Agreement

- Begin with an introductory statement of the issues being mediated.

- If necessary, take a break to do the fine tuning and prepare a draft text. Use only one copy for revisions.

- Include steps for follow-up and review.

- Have parties read it, make corrections and ensure both sides agree (do not re-open the negotiations, ask only for comments on accuracy and for approval).

- Ask parties to sign and give each a copy.

What to Remember when Writing Agreements

- Use simple language.

- Avoid any mention of blame, fault or guilt.

- Avoid jargon.

- Identify people by full names.

- Ensure consistency by:
  - accurately reflecting what parties agree to do.
  - being consistent and avoiding words which mean different things, or, using two or more words which mean the same thing.
  - listing each provision separately.

- Avoid ambiguity by:
  - choosing descriptive adjectives carefully.
  - specifying who, where, what, when, how.
  - writing out dollar figures and method of payment.
  - ensuring that definitions are understood.
  - not involving other people in the agreement.

The key is to be aware of prejudices so we can put them aside

Prejudice and Bias

Most mediators at some time struggle with feelings of bias. Most can recognize these feelings and try to put them aside. A firm inner decision to cope can empower mediators to handle situations which at first seem sensitive. Mediation requires that the mediators be able to temporarily put aside personal opinions and feelings in order to work with people on their own terms. Mediators need to understand the limits of their abilities to stay impartial, and in some instances may have to decide not to mediate a certain case.

Value differences, prejudices and feelings can bias a mediator in three areas: 1) the agreement, 2) impartiality, and 3) their relationship with a co-mediator.

When mediators are biased, they may pay less than full attention to a disputant or conversely, they may lean over too far trying to be fair. Mediators may be drawn to disputants who talk easily, cooperate with the mediation process, show willingness to compromise or apologize, or to those who dress appropriately or look attractive. Sometimes the difficulty is not with particular disputants, but with the particular situation or dispute.

Power in Conflict

All of us have power over others and all of us give power to others.

Power (personal, rather than structural) is the ability to influence other people or groups. Power is inherent in all human interaction, especially conflict. It can be used to dominate others, or to enhance a sense of our own power. Power comes from such things as size, money, age, status, gender, class and culture – to name a few.

The key to assessing power is to understand how it is used. Awareness of our own power is basic to our interaction with others.

If we are not intimidated by threats or manipulated by authority, then these power sources will not have power over us. It is important to become aware of our power resources, especially the power we give to others.
We are striving to have power with (collaborate), rather than power over (compete).

Power Imbalance

A mediator should refuse to mediate cases where significant power imbalances would undermine the mediation process, or if their competence level is incapable of dealing with differences in power.

Mediation presumes the parties are able to negotiate on relatively equal terms. When they are not, power imbalance occurs. People can feel overpowered as a result of physical size, money, age, race, authority, gender or verbal skills. When this happens, the stronger party may begin to believe that they are going to "win" by stonewalling or wearing down the other person. Weaker parties may feel that there is no use, they will lose anyway. There may also be times that one party does not really want to resolve the issue (they may have something to gain from continuing the conflict).

Power imbalances are difficult to deal with, but there are ways of lessening their impact. One way is to ensure that each party has roughly equal time to tell their story and state their interests. A second way is to slow down the process and help the weaker party explain their concerns. Sometimes a simple thing like moving closer or changing your tone of voice can be comforting to a weaker person. Without the mediator's support, the weaker party may have little motivation to continue working toward a solution. Whichever way the mediator chooses to support the weaker party, they must always be fair and trustworthy to both parties or they will lose their impartial status.

Screening of cases to identify power imbalances is very important. Power imbalance can jeopardize reaching a fair outcome, or can harm one of the parties. A mediator should refuse to mediate cases where significant power imbalances would undermine the mediation process, or if their competence level is incapable of dealing with differences in power.

Anger

Anger is a natural emotion but a difficult feeling to deal with in conflict situations. It is important to know that anger is a legitimate feeling and that it is OK to be angry. When used properly, anger can enhance our lives, give us energy and strength and tell us something is wrong or needs attention. When we do not understand our anger we react in a misdirected way and become less productive.

We encounter anger in various forms. When we are treated unfairly we feel hurt. On the other hand, when we assertively right a wrong we feel proud. Anger is a secondary emotion often triggered by the emotion of fear.

Stages of Anger

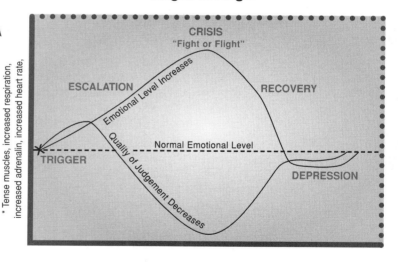

Trigger Stage
As we begin to feel emotionally or physically threatened by an external event or internally our physiological system begins to prepare for it.

Escalation Stage
Our body prepares by pumping adrenalin into the blood stream causing: increased respiration (rapid breathing); increased heart rate and raised blood pressure; tense muscles (jaw, neck, shoulders, hands); voice pitch to alter and get louder; eyes change (pupils enlarge, brow falls).

Crisis Stage
This stage requires a "fight or flight" decision. Unfortunately, our quality of judgement is low and decisions are not made with our best reasoning.

Recovery Stage
After action is taken the body begins to recover. Adrenalin does not leave the blood stream at once and it takes time for normal levels to be reached. Quality of judgement begins to return.

Post-Crisis Depression Stage
The body enters a short period when the heart rate slips below normal. Awareness and energy return. Assessment of what occurred often leads to feelings of guilt, regret and depression.

Managing the Emotional Climate

At a minimum, mediators must ensure that the parties do not leave the mediation session in worse shape than when they came in. It is hoped that the parties will learn to negotiate difficult emotional issues with increased self-control and respect for the other person.

It is much easier for the mediator to prevent the parties from losing control than it is to regain control once it is lost. Mediators need to be directive and intervene immediately to deal with accusatory, blaming, critical statements. It is very important to be supportive and acknowledge the valid angry feelings before redirecting the destructive angry behaviour.

The following interventions can be used to maintain a safe environment. Mediator's judgment is required to determine the appropriateness of the intervention.

1. **Ignore**
   The event may not require intervention particularly if it is minimal or not heard by the other party.

2. **Body Language**
   Use body orientation or gesture to intervene.

3. **Acknowledgement**
   "You're very angry and that tells me how important this issue is to you."

4. **Normalize**
   "When people get angry or feel defensive, it is very typical for them to interrupt. If you can hold back your comments until Ann is finished, it will make it easier to hear each other. I will ensure you get the opportunity to respond."

5. **Educate**
   "Words like idiot create defensiveness. John just sat back in his chair and looked away. Is there any way you can tell him, more neutrally, what you're thinking and feeling?"

6. **Consequence**
   "I'm wondering if the two of you have argued like this in the past. What happens when you begin arguing?"

7. **Venting**
   Encourage rational versus emotional discussion. *"Suzanne, a few minutes ago, it seemed that what John was saying was really triggering and upsetting you. Perhaps you can tell him what you are reacting to."*

8. **Confronting**
   To help the participants gain insight into how their behaviour is preventing them from moving ahead to the attainment of a viable agreement. *"When you are saying you are angry, you talk to me, not Suzanne, and you're also smiling. I'm confused about how you are feeling.*

9. **Ask Them To Give You Suggestions**
   "Can you think of some ways that would help the two of you listen to each other rather than talk at the same time?"

10. **Call A Break**
    "Perhaps it would be useful for us to take a 15 minute break in order for you to cool down."

11. **Recognize Difficulty of the Issue and Point Out Progress**
    "This hasn't been easy and you've been working very hard."

12. **Suggest That Parties Take Notes and Write Down Their Ideas, Positions, Disagreements**
    So as to remember them and not have parties interrupt each other.

Co-Mediation

Co-mediation involves two mediators who work as a team. Co-mediation provides many benefits:

- It is easier to listen and observe when freed from the active mediator role.

- Mediating is intense and can be physically, intellectually and emotionally draining; co-mediating lightens the load.

- Co-mediators may be chosen to reflect attributes of the disputants (gender, profession, ethnic background), which often helps the parties feel at ease.

- Co-mediation demonstrates cooperative teamwork in action. When one mediator is unsure of how to proceed or wants to check out an idea he or she can turn to the co-mediator. This enhances the process, alleviates pressure, and models cooperation.

- Co-mediating can provide invaluable training for an inexperienced mediator. More experienced mediators can "mentor" less experienced or less confident mediators.

- Co-mediation provides an opportunity to evaluate a particular case, as well as an opportunity to give and receive feedback on mediation skills.

How to Co-mediate

■ Prepare ahead – do not try to co-mediate by the "seat of your pants".

■ Discuss your strengths and weaknesses. Look for ways that you can support each other and learn new skills.

■ Decide how the responsibilities will be divided (stages, tasks, issues).

■ Discuss what strategies you will use; how to change strategies during mediation; and how to interrupt each other without causing tension.

■ Work out the signals you plan to use.

■ Be sure both of you speak early in the session to obtain some "voice legitimacy".

■ Discuss balance – one mediator should not dominate and the other be a silent "wall flower".

■ Develop a strategy on how to work together and how to keep each other on track to avoid one of you "taking the ball into left field".

■ Work out internal dispute resolution procedures. (Disputants do not need a conflict between their mediators.)

Functions of a Mediator

People can be intimidated by a face-to-face encounter. A mediator is sensitive to this and provides realistic hope and encouragement that the problem can be resolved.

Regulate Interaction

This includes the physical location and seating arrangements. A mediator is responsible for setting the tone of the meeting, establishing guidelines, ordering the discussion, and controlling emotional outbursts, insults, and criticism. The overall purpose is to minimize the amount of threat experienced by the parties and ensure that each has a fair mediation session.

Aid Communication

A mediator ensures each party understands the other's thoughts and feelings and assists them in hearing and talking to one another.

Monitor the Process

While participating actively, the mediator must also take time to analyze what is happening. A mediator needs to be conscious of perceived power imbalances, whether real or not.

A Mediator Needs to Know

- What can and cannot be mediated
- How to obtain a commitment to mediate
- The difference between issues and interests
- Their personal limits
- The moral and legal issues and implications
- The difference between mediation and other ADR processes the stages of mediation
- Appropriate ground rules
- Something about the substantive area of the case
- When and how to involve other available referral sources.

A Mediator Needs to be Able to...

- Listen, attend, observe, give feedback
- Respond accurately and sensitively to feelings and situations
- Identify and prioritize relevant issues
- Describe behaviour in concrete and non-judgemental terms
- Identify underlying needs and interests
- Effectively use questions and confrontation
- Express parties' agreements clearly, verbally and in writing
- Describe and manage the mediation process
- Maintain a safe environment
- Minimize power imbalances
- Co-mediate and evaluate a mediation session.

Hallmarks of an Advanced Practitioner

Being a skilled mediator requires the integration of skills, knowledge and self-reflection. The following are some hallmarks of advanced mediation practice.

Knowledge and Skills

- mediation it is not just about process; it requires skill, knowledge, assessment, timing, intuition, empathy, judgment, risk, patience, confidence

- able to assume the many roles of a mediator

Critical Mind

- can distinguish their orientation from other mediation approaches

- takes time to reflect on how a mediation could have been improved

- assesses the possible good and harm that could come out of a mediation

- knows when it is time to consult or bring in the experts

- knows when it is time to terminate the mediation

Flexible / Creative / Inquisitive

- willing to change their style of mediation to accommodate parties needs and abilities
- incorporates humor, metaphor, drama, drawing, language, sculpting and other creative tools to help parties present their point of view, understand each other and continue negotiating
- stays curious and non-judgmental

Reflective

- recognizes personal limits, biases, values, world views
- is in touch with and can manage own emotions
- is able to "think outside the box"

Lifelong Learner

- is familiar with developments in theory and research in the field
- reads books, academic journals and professional newsletters
- frequently attends professional conferences, workshops and courses
- is a member of professional associations
- networks with other professionals in the field

Temptations for Mediators

- Have the answers.
- Give advice.
- Take sides.
- Use sloppy or indirect language.
- Fill in the silence.
- Equate success with getting an agreement.
- Keep things heated up.
- Keep the lid on things.

Mediator's Checklist

- What strengths do I have?

- Do I share the session easily with other mediators?

- When do I have trouble staying impartial and how do I handle it?

- How do I react to open conflict and hostility?

- Do I slip into other roles: advisor, counsellor, judge, advocate, comforter?

- Is my language clear? How often do I use silence?

- How do I react to differences between me and the disputants (ie. class, race, education, age, gender?)

- What signals or comments have I picked up about my mediating from the disputants?

- Do I evaluate with my co-mediator following a session?

- Do I ask for and accept criticism from my co-mediators?

Bibliography

Abel, Richard L., *The Politics of Informal Justice*, 2 Vols. New York: Academic Press, 1982

Auerbach, Jerold, S., *Justice Without Law? Resolving Disputes Without Lawyers.* New York: Oxford University Press, 1983

Avruch, K. & P. Black, "Conflict resolution in intercultural settings: Problems and prospects," in Sandole and Vander Merwe (eds.) *Conflict Resolution Theory and Practice.* New York: Manchester University Press, 1993

Boardman, Susan and Horowitz, Sandra, "Constructive Conflict Management and Social Problems: An Introduction," *Journal of Social Issues*, Vol. 50, No. 1, 1994:1-12

Bunker, Barbara Benedict, Rubin, Jeffery, Z., and Associates, *Conflict, Cooperation and Justice.* San Francisco: Jossey-Bass Publishers, 1995

Bush, R.B., and Folger, J., *The Promise of Mediation.* San Francisco: Jossey Bass, 1994

Bush, R.B., "What Do We Need a Mediator For?: Mediation's "Value-Added" for Negotiators," *Ohio State Journal on Dispute Resolution* Vol. 12 No.1, 1996

Carnevale, P.J., Lim, R.G., and Mclaughlin, M.E., "Contingent Mediator Behavior and Its Effectiveness in K. Kressel, D. Pruitt, and Associates, *Mediation Research*. San Francisco: Jossey-Bass, 1989:213-240

Cook,R.F., Roehl, J.A., and Sheppard, D. *Neighbourhood Justice Center Field Test: Final Evaluation Report*. 1980.

Coser, Lewis, *The Functions of Social Conflict*. New York: Free Press, 1956

Coser, Lewis, *Continuities in the Study of Social Conflict*. New York: Free Press, 1968

Department of Justice Canada, *Dispute Resolution in Canada: A Survey of Activities and Services*. Ottawa, 1995

Deutsch, Morton, *The Resolution of Conflict*. Hew Haven: Yale University Press, 1973

Deutsch, Morton, "Constructive Conflict Resolution: Principles, Training, and Research," *Journal of Social Issues*, Vol. 50 No. 1, 1994:13-32

Fisher, R. and W. Ury, *Getting to Yes*. Boston: Houghton Mifflin Co., 1981

Folberg, Jay, and Taylor, Allison, *Mediation: A Comprehensive Guide to Resolving Conflicts Without Litigation*. San Francisco: Jossey Bass, 1990

Fuller, Lon, "Mediation Its Forms and Functions," *Southern California Law Review* Vol. 44, 1971

Garrett, R.D., "Mediation in Native America," *Dispute Resolution Journal*, March 1994:38-45

Golberg, S., Green, E. & Sander, F. *Dispute Resolution*. Boston: Little, Brown & Company, 1985

Harrington, C.B., *Shadow Justice? The Ideology and Institutionalization of Alternatives to Court*. Westport and London: Greenwood Press, 1985

Harrington, Christine B. and Merry Sally Engel, "Ideological Production: The Making of Community Mediation". *Law and Society Review*, Vol. 22, No., 1988:709-735

Himes, Joseph, "The Nature of Social Conflict," in *Conflict and Conflict Management*. Athens: The University of Georgia Press, 1980:2-26

Hocker, Joyce and Wilmot, William, *Interpersonal Conflict*. Madison: WCB Brown and Benchmark, 1995

Hofrichter, Richard, *Neighbourhood Justice in Capitalist Society: The Expansion of the Informal State*. New York: Greenwood Press, 1987

Hofstede, G., *Culture's Consequences: International Differences in Work-Related Values*. Beverley Hills: Sage Publications, 1980

Jaffe, Sanford, "The Adversary System: Is there a better way?" National Institute for Dispute Resolution: Washington, 1983

Katz, Neil and Lawyer, John, *Conflict Resolution: Building Bridges*. Thousand Oaks: Corwin Press, 1993

Kolb, D.M., *The Mediators*. Cambridge: The MIT Press, 1983

Kolb, D.M., *When Talk Works: Profiles of Mediators*. San Francisco: Jossey Bass, 1994

Kressel, K., Pruitt, D., and Associates, *Mediation Research*. Centre for Negotiation and Conflict Resolution at Rutgers, State University of New Jersey, 1989

Kruk, Edward, *Mediation and Conflict Resolution in Social Work and the Human Services*. Chicago: Nelson Hall, 1997

Lajeunesse, T., and Woods, A., *Mediation Services: An Evaluation*. Manitoba Attorney General Research Planning, and Evaluation, 1987

LeBaron, Michelle, "Intercultural Disputes: Mediation, Conflict Resolution, and Multicultural Reality: Culturally Competent Practice," in Edward Kruk,(ed.) *Mediation and Conflict Resolution in Social Work and the Human Services*. Chicago: Nelson Hall, 1997:315-335

Lederach, John Paul, *Beyond Prescription: New Lenses for Conflict Resolution across Cultures*. Waterloo: Institute of Peace and Conflict Studies – Conrad Grebel College, 1992

Mcfarlane, Julie, "Court-Based Mediation for Civil Cases: an Evaluation of the Ontario Court (General Division) ADR Centre," 1995

Mcfarlane, Julie, *Rethinking Disputes: The Mediation Alternative*. Toronto: Emond Montgomery, 1997

Merry, Sally Engle, "Myth and Practice in the Mediation Process," in Wright and Galaway, *Mediation and Criminal Justice*. Newbury Park: Sage Publications, 1989

Moore, Christopher, W., *The Mediation Process: Practical Strategies for Resolving Conflict*. San Francisco: Jossey-Bass Publishers, 1986

Nader, Laura, "Harmony Models and the Construction of Law," in Avruch, Black and Scimecca (eds.) *Conflict Resolution: Cross Cultural Perspectives*. Westport: Greenwood Press, 1991:41-59

NIDR, National Institute for Dispute Resolution, "Statement of Madeleine Crohn, Before the U.S. House of Representatives Subcommittee on Intellectual Property and Judicial Administration, May 19, 1992" in *Forum*, Summer 1992

Ontario Civil Justice Review, *Supplemental and Final Report*. Toronto: Publications Ontario, November 1996

Picard, C.A., "The Emergence of Mediation as a Profession," in C. Morris and A. Pirie (eds.), *Qualifications for Dispute Resolution*. Victoria: UVic Institute for Dispute Resolution, 1994: 141-164

Porter, J. and Taplin, R., "Means of Conflict Resolution," in *Conflict and Conflict Resolution*. New York: University Press of America, 1987: 19-35

Riskin, L., "Understanding Mediator Orientations, Strategies and Techniques: A Grid for the Perplexed," *Harvard Negotiation Law Review* Vol. 7, 1996:25-35

Riskin, Leonard and Westbrook, James, *Dispute Resolution and Lawyers.* St. Paul: West Publishing, 1987

Roehl, J. and Cook, R., "Mediation in Interpersonal Disputes: Effectiveness and Limitations", in K. Kressel, D. Pruitt and Associates, *Mediation Research.* San Francisco: Jossey Bass, 1989 pp. 31-52

Scimecca, Joseph, Theory and alternative dispute resolution: a contradiction in terms?" in D. Sandole and H. van der Merwe, *Conflict Resolution Theory and Practice.* 1993: 211-221

Schwerin, Edward, W., *Mediation, Citizen Empowerment and Transformational Politics.* Westport: Praeger, 1995: 93-108

Silbey, Susan and Merry, Sally, "Mediator Settlement Strategies," *Law and Policy* Vol. 8 No. 1 January 1986

Spitzer, Steven, "The Dialectics of Formal and Informal Control" in R. Abel, *The Politics of Informal Justice Vol. 1.* New York: Academic Press pp. 167-201, 1982

Stulberg, Joseph, B., *Taking Charge/Managing Conflict.* New York: Lexington, 1987

Thomas, Kenneth and Kilmann, Ralph, "Thomas-Kilmann Conflict Mode Instrument". Xicom, 1974

Tomasic, R. and Freeley, M., *Neighbourhood Justice: Assessment of an Emerging Idea.* New York: Longman, 1982

Umbreit, Mark, "Mediation of Criminal Conflict: An Assessment of Programs in Four Canadian Provinces," Ottawa: Department of Justice, 1995

Waldman, Ellen, "The Challenge of Certification: How to Ensure Mediator Competence While Preserving Diversity," *University of San Francisco Law Review*, Vol. 30 Spring 1996

Wall, J. Jr., and Lynn, A., "Mediation: A Current Review," *Journal of Conflict Resolution*, Vol. 37 No. 1, March 1993:160-194

Wright, Martin, "Introduction", in *Mediation and Criminal Justice: Victims, Offenders and Community.* Newbury Park, Cal. 91320: Sage Publications, 1989

Zuber, T.G. The Honourable, *Report of the Ontario Courts Inquiry.* Toronto: Ministry of the Attorney General, 1987

National Organizations

The Network: Interaction for Conflict Resolution (The Network)
Conrad Grebel College
Waterloo, Ontario N2L 3G6
Phone: (519) 885-0880

Family Mediation Canada (FMC)
123 Woolwich Street
Guelph, Ontario N1E 2V2
Phone: (519) 836-7750

Society for Professionals in Dispute Resolution (SPIDR)
1621 Connecticut Ave NW Suite 400
Washington D.C. 20036
Phone: (202) 833-2188

National Institute for Dispute Resolution (NIDR)
1726 M Street NW, Suite 500
Washington, D.C. 20036
Phone: (202) 466-4764
Fax: (202) 466-4769
E-mail: nidr@nidr.org

Arbitration and Mediation Institute of Canada (AMIC)
Suite 2600 – 160 Elgin Street
Ottawa, Ontario K1P 1C3
Contact Robert Nelson / Brigitte Raymond
Phone: (613) 786-8650
Fax: (613) 563-9869

Suggested Readings

Bishop, Peter, *Winning in the Workplace.* Scarborough: Carswell, 1995

Bush, R. and Folger, J., *The Promise of Mediation.* San Francisco: Jossey Bass 1994

Duffy, K., Grosch, J. and Olczak, P., *Community Mediation: A Handbook for Practicioners and Researchers.* New York: Guilford Press, 1991.

Folberg, J., & Taylor, A., *Mediation: A Comprehensive Guide to Resolving Conflicts Without Litigation.* San Francisco: Jossey-Bass Publishers 1990

Folger, J. and Jones, T. *New Directions in Mediation.* California: Sage Publications 1994

Grey, Barbara, *Collaborating: Finding Common Ground for MultiParty Problems.* San Francisco: Jossey-Bass Publishers 1989

Hoffman, Ben, *Conflict Power Persuasion: Negotiating Effectively.* North York: Captus Press Inc. 1990

Irving, H. and Benjamin, M., *Family Mediation Contemporary Issues.* Thousand Oaks: Sage Publications, 1995.

Jandt, Fred, *Win-Win Negotiating: Turning Conflict into Agreement.* Toronto: John Wiley & Sons 1985

Kressel, K. Pruitt, D. & Assoc., *Mediation Research.* San Francisco: Jossey-Bass Publishers 1989

Kruk, Edward (ed), *Mediation and Conflict Resolution in Social Work and the Human Services.* Chicago: Nelson Hall, 1997

MacFarlane, Julie (ed), *Rethinking Disputes: The Mediation Alternative.* Toronto: Emond Montgomery, 1997

Mediation Quarterly, a journal published by Jossey-Bass, San Francisco

Morris, C. and Pirie, A. (eds), *Qualifications for Dispute Resolution: Perspectives on the Debate.* Victoria: UVic Institute for Dispute Resolution 1994

Moore, Christopher, *The Mediation Process.* San Francisco: Jossey-Bass Publishers 1986

Negotiation Journal, published by the Program on Negotiation. Harvard Law School.

Robert, Marc, *Managing Conflict From The Inside Out.* San Diego: University Assoc. 1982

Schwarz, Roger. *The Skilled Facilitator.* San Francisco: Jossey-Bass Publishers 1994

Ury, William, *Getting Past No.* New York: Bantam 1991

Weisbord, Marvin R., *Productive Workplaces.* Jossey-Bass Publishers, San Francisco, 1989

Glossary of Terms

Active Listening
Making an effort to hear, understand and demonstrate understanding of what is said and felt.

Adjudication
A formal process conducted by a judge or jury in a court of law. Decisions are reached on points of law, rather than on moral right or wrong.

Alternative Dispute Resolution (ADR)
Processes other than those most commonly used to deal with disputes. ADR processes attempt to reduce the delay and high costs, financial and emotional, commonly associated with litigation.

Arbitration
Binding settlement of a dispute by an impartial third party.

Assertiveness
The ability to state one's views positively, without aggression.

Brainstorm
To freely share suggestions or ideas without discussion or evaluation.

CHEAP BFVs
Interests that reflect concerns, hopes, expectations, assumptions, priorities, beliefs, fears and values.

Compromise
The process of mutual concession to resolve differences.

Conciliation
A neutral third party, with no decision-making power, acts as a go-between with the disputing parties to arrive at a solution to the problem. Parties usually do not meet together.

Conflict
A problem or disagreement between two or more people.

Conflict Management
The use of problem-solving and communication skills to change potentially destructive conflict into constructive conflict. It promotes mutual understanding and agreeable action strategies and can result in the resolution of disagreement or a willingness to live with differences.

Escalation
To increase the magnitude or intensity of conflict, making resolution more difficult.

Mediation
A voluntary process for settling disputes in which an acceptable, impartial third party, who has no authoritative decision-making power, helps the disputing parties reach a mutually satisfactory agreement.

Negotiation
Discussion between two parties with a view to reaching agreement without assistance from a third party.

Ombudsperson
A third party who investigates and expedites complaints with the goal of settling the complaint or proposing changes.

Reframing
The process of changing how a person defines or conceptualizes a particular situation or event.

Role Play
A learning technique where two or more people act out scripts of other people.

Sample

Mediation Agreement

We, the undersigned, have authority to enter into an agreement between:

_____ and _____ .

In an attempt to resolve a dispute, we agree to the following terms and conditions:

Action and Person Responsible   Timeframe

1.

2.

3.

4.

_____   _____
            (Party A)   (Party B)

_____
            (Mediator)

Dated at _____ , this _____ day of _____ , 199___.

Standards of Practice

Family Mediation Canada

Practice Guidelines for Competent Family Mediators

These practice guidelines, approved in 1996, set out uniform national standars for family mediators across Canada.

Competent family mediators shall work with the participants to establish and maintain a mediation process that will:

1. be client centered;

2. facilitate the participants' involvement in the mediation while taking into consideration their respective:

   a) abilities to negotiate;

   b) abilities to make decisions in accordance with their own individual interests;

   c) powers to influence family decision making;

   d) psychological, emotional and economic states;

   e) access to and understandings of relevant information; and

   f) access to appropriate support services such as independent legal advice;

3. ensure that the participants have adequate time to fully discuss and to attempt to resolve their disputes and conflicts;

4. ensure that families with histories of abuse or unmanageable power imbalances are assessed for appropriateness of mediation and are referred to other services if necessary;

5. ensure that culturally appropriate forms of dispute resolution may be considered and included where appropriate;

6. ensure that the interest of all persons having a personal interest in the dispute or conflict are considered;

7. ensure confidentiality of the process is maintained except when:

   a) the family mediator suspects that a child is in need of protection;

   b) the mediator determines there is a need to inform a potential victim and the police about an imminent danger;

   c) there is a mutual agreement that the information may be released, as in an open mediation;

d) the mediator may need to breech confidentiality in order to comply with a duty to disclose the whereabouts of a child in cases of abduction;

8. use language which is meaningful and appropriate to the participants' level of understanding;

9. be equitable to all people;

10. recognize the special interests of children and ensure these will be considered in parental agreements;

11. assist people to resolve family problems in a way that respects each family's interests, values, and rights to self-determination, while also respecting the interests and rights of others who may be affected;

12. be sensitive to the participants' cultural needs and understanding of fairness;

13. ensure that agreements reached in mediation reflect the range of options considered acceptable in law and in the event that the participants wish to enter an agreement falling outside that range of options, mediators shall encourage the participants to obtain independent legal advice and to reflect for a period of time before concluding the agreement; and

14. attempt to ensure that no one suffers physical or emotional abuse as a result of participating in mediation.

The Tasks of a Competent Family Mediator
Pre-Mediation Tasks

1. Receive and read case file and information for intake when appropriate;

2. Encourage and, in appropriate circumstances, require participants to obtain independent legal advice prior to or at the beginning of the mediation process;

3. Assess for the appropriateness of mediation and refer cases to other services unless the mediator can ensure that;

   a) there is/has been no family abuse, or that the abuse that occurred in the past will not affect mediation negatively;

   b) that he/she will comply fully with FMC's Code of Professional Conduct;

c) s/he can put into place all safety measures that may be required for the protection of the mediator, mediation staff and all participants;

d) imbalances in power or the negotiating abilities of the participants can be managed by the mediator in a way that ensures the full and equitable participation of all participants; and

e) s/he has the education, training and expertise required to mediate the conflict completely;

4. If the mediation is inappropriate, make referrals to other services and terminate mediation safely;

5. Assess for participants' readiness to mediate and, in particular, ensure that, for the foreseeable future, reconciliation is not possible;

6. Refer the participants to reconciliation or marital counseling when appropriate;

7. Review the mediation process and the parameters of confidentiality with the participants;

8. Reach an agreement with the participants regarding rules for sharing and withholding of information divulged separately by each participant to the mediator in caucus or otherwise;

9. Disclose the mediator's biases and any conflicts of interest;

10. Help the participants identify all those interested in or affected by the conflict;

11. Be sensitive to cultural maters that may affect the mediation process and help the participants develop dispute resolution process that is sensitive to culture; and

12. Sign and "Agreement to Mediate" or a "Mediation Retainer Contract."

Core Family Mediation Tasks

1. **Establish an empathic, effective working relationship with the participants**, and in particular:

    a) maintain impartiality and objectivity;

    b) build rapport and trust through demonstration of understanding of the participants;

c)   enhance the quality of the participants' communication with each other;

d)   set a cooperative tone;

e)   promote each participant's understanding of the conflict and enhance each participant's insight into and empathy for the views and personal situations of the other;

f)   encourage and support self-empowerment of the participants;

g)   respect the participants' self-determination;

h)   be sensitive to culture as it relates to the process;

i)   manage the emotional climate (particularly feelings associated with the experience of separation and divorce for adults and children);

j)   encourage the participants throughout the process;

k)   refocus the participants on the needs of the children in cases where this is applicable;

l)   maintain safety and terminate the mediation if anyone's safety cannot be assured;

m)   create an environment of mutual exploration;

n)   speak in a way the participants can understand and assist the participants to do likewise;

o)   identify the participants' values;

p)   facilitate and model active listening;

q)   obtain and process information from the participants;

r)   manage power imbalances throughout the process; and

s)   use neutral interpreters when necessary.

2.   **Facilitate the Participants' Negotiations and Resolutions**, in particular:

a)   ensure that the participants understand and are satisfied with the structure and form of the conflict resolution process;

b)   guide the participants through the mediation process;

c)   assess when to make appropriate changes in the process (such as when to: bring in partisan support for participants having difficulty dealing with power or negotiation imbalances, include experts in mediation for information purposes, include children or stepparents or extended family members, employ individual or group caucuses, refer participants to other professionals or procedures for information or support) and negotiate changes in procedure with the participants;

d)   facilitate the full disclosure of all information relevant to the dispute;

e)   maintain a productive present and future focus (focus on the past only when helpful to participants in their efforts to resolve the conflict);

f)   when dealing with families separating or divorcing, seek information from the participants about the impact of separation and divorce in their family;

g)   whenever appropriate, provide information to the participants about the impact and effect of separation and divorce on parents and children;

h)   guide the participants' discussions from positions to interests;

I)   help the participants develop options and evaluate their feasibility;

j)   ensure the participants understand the options available to them if agreement is not reached;

k)   ensure the participants measure solutions against criteria of fairness and the interests of all affected others;

l)   work with the participants to enable them to implement any decision or agreement;

m)   draft a concluding document that will record the results of the mediation;

n)   strongly encourage participants to seek independent legal advice before concluding mediation and before signing any concluding document if legal issues are involved;

o)   make referrals, when appropriate, to specialists, other services and other sources of information;

p)   determine when, if and how the mediator must withdraw from mediation, acting always in accordance with the FMC Code of Professional Conduct;

q)   assist the participants to create a plan (such as returning to mediation at a later date or utilizing other dispute resolution processes) to resolve issues which have not been settled in mediation; and

r)   adhere to FMC's Professional Code of Conduct.

• • • • • • • • • • • •

SPIDR
Society of Professionals
in Dispute Resolution

SPIDR'S Ethical Standards
of Professional Responsibility
Adopted June 1986

Introduction

The Society of Professionals in Dispute Resolution (SPIDR) was established in 1973 to promote the peaceful resolution of disputes. Members of the Society believe that resolving disputes through negotiation, mediation, arbitration and other neutral interventions can be of great benefit to disputing parties and to society. In 1983, the SPIDR Board of Directors charged the SPIDR Ethics Committee with the task of developing ethical standards of professional responsibility. The committee membership represented all the various sectors and disciplines within SPIDR. This document, adopted by the Board on June 2, 1986, is the result of that charge.

The purpose of this document is to promote among SPIDR Members and Associates ethical conduct and a high level of competency among SPIDR Members, including honesty, integrity, impartiality and the exercise of good judgment in their dispute resolution efforts. It is hoped that this document also will help to (1) define the profession of dispute resolution, (2) educate the public, and (3) inform users of dispute resolution services.

Application of Standards

Adherence to these ethical standards by SPIDR Members and Associates is basic to professional responsibility. SPIDR Members and Associates commit themselves to be guided in their professional conduct by these standards. The SPIDR Board of Directors or its designee is available to advise members and Associates about the interpretation of these standards. Other neutral practitioners and organizations are welcome to follow these standards.

Scope

It is recognized that SPIDR Members and Associates resolve disputes in various sectors within the disciplines of dispute resolution and have their own codes of professional conduct. These standards have been developed as general guideline of practice for neutral disciplines represented in the SPIDR membership. Ethical considerations relevant to some, but not to all, of these disciplines are not covered by these standards.

General Responsibilities

Neutrals have a duty to the parties, to the profession, and to themselves. They should be honest and unbiased, act in good faith, be diligent, and not seek to advance their own interests at the expense of their parties'.

Neutrals must act fairly in dealing with the parties, have no personal interest in the terms of the settlement, show no bias toward individuals and institutions involved in the dispute, be reasonably available as requested by the parties, and be certain that the parties are informed of the process in which they are involved.

Responsibilities to the Parties

Impartiality. The neutral must maintain impartiality toward all parties. Impartiality means freedom from favoritism or bias either by word or by action, and a commitment to serve all parties as opposed to a single party.

Informed Consent. The neutral has an obligation to assure that all parties understand the nature of the process, the procedures, the particular role of the neutral, and the parties' relationship to the neutral.

Confidentiality. Maintaining confidentiality is critical to the dispute resolution process. Confidentiality encourages candor, a full exploration of the issues, and a neutral's acceptability. There may be some types of cases, however, in which confidentiality is not protected. In such cases, the neutral must advise the parties, when appropriate in the dispute resolution process, that the confidentiality of the proceedings cannot necessarily be maintained. Except in such instances, the neutral must resist all attempts to cause him or her to reveal any information outside the process. A commitment by the neutral to hold information in confidence within the process also must be honored.

Conflict of Interest. The neutral must refrain from entering or continuing in any dispute if he or she believes or perceives that participation as a neutral would be a clear conflict of interest and any circumstances that may reasonably raise a question as to the neutral's impartiality.

The duty to disclose is a continuing obligation throughout the process.

Promptness. The neutral shall exert every reasonable effort to expedite the process.

The Settlement and Its Consequences. The dispute resolution process belongs to the parties. The neutral has no vested interest in the terms of a settlement, but must be satisfied that agreements in which he or she has participated will not impugn the integrity of the process. The neutral has a responsibility to see that the parties consider the terms of a settlement. If the neutral is concerned about the possible consequences of a proposed agreement, and the needs of the parties dictate, the neutral must inform the parties of that concern. In adhering to this standard, the neutral may find is advisable to educate the parties, to refer one or more parties for specialized advise, or to withdraw from the case. In no case, however, shall the neutral violate section 3, Confidentiality, of these standards.

Unrepresented Interests

The neutral must consider circumstances where interests are not represented in the process. The neutral has an obligation, where in his or her judgment the needs of parties dictate, to assure that such interest have been considered by the principal parties.

Use of Multiple Procedures

The use of more than one dispute resolution procedure by the same neutral involves additional responsibilities. Where the use of more than one procedure is initially contemplated, the neutral must take care at the outset to advice the parties of the nature of the procedures and the consequences of revealing information during any one procedure which the neutral may later use for decision making or may share with another decision maker. Where the use of more that one procedure is contemplated after the initiation of the dispute resolution process, the neutral must explain the consequences and afford the parties an opportunity to select another neutral for the subsequent procedures. It is also incumbent upon the neutral to advise the parties of the transition from one dispute resolution process to another.

Background and Qualifications

A neutral should accept responsibility only in cases where the neutral has sufficient knowledge regarding the appropriate process and subject matter to be affective. A neutral has a responsibility to maintain and improve his or her professional skills.

Disclosure of Fees

It is the duty of the neutral to explain to the parties at the outset of the process the bases of compensation, fees and charges, if any.

Support of the Profession

The experienced neutral should participate in the development of new practitioners in the field and engage in efforts to educate the public about the value and use of neutral dispute resolution procedures. The neutral should provide *pro bono* service, where appropriate.

Responsibilities of Neutrals Working on the Same Case

In the event that more than one neutral is involved in the resolution of a dispute, each has an obligation to inform the others regarding his or her entry in the case. Neutrals working with the same parties should maintain an open and professional relationship with each other.

Advertising and Solicitation

A neutral must be aware that some forms of advertising and solicitations are inappropriate and in some conflict resolution disciplines, such as labor arbitration, are impermissible. All advertising must honestly represent the services to be rendered. No claims of specific results or promises which imply favor of one side or another for the purpose of obtaining business should be made. No commissions, rebates, or another similar forms of remuneration should be given or received by a neutral for the referral of clients.